From "Oh, My Redwood Heart!"

Finally, as the summer came to a close, one evening Phil and I sat talking, and I told him, "I've never had anyone make love to me." "Oh!" He was surprised. Well, I was in my late 20s, I had the look of a casual hippy girl, and I wasn't religious like my Grandmother or his own family. Anyone would assume I was experienced; at least, I hoped so, for this was a secret I'd never told anyone before.
Then I asked Phil, "Would you make love to me?"

Histories of love, of thoughts and inventions, lives of others, from those you meet once to those you love forever, and one whole life of your own, all this and more fit into the universe of the brain.... how preciously fragile the brain's universe and the human's life can be, nature-made from the beginning and subject to infinitesimal pluses and minuses of health and chance. So many elements go into the making of a life that it hurts to know.

More Reviews of "Oh, My Redwood Heart!"

To the author from Debbie Sjoberg: *You have the ability to write in your own voice, which is concise, direct, and effortlessly poetic. Many pages were good for me, personally, because they were so uplifting to the reader and transcended your times of sadness. I really loved your observation of the 7-year cycles in life, and it was fun to think back and see if that worked in my life, too. It does! This is a good year to be publishing your book, and I agree that 62 will be a momentous age for both of us.*

"This luminous story of Phil and Debbie's marriage, about the joyful times as well as the struggles with mental illness, only confirms the fact: Love Transforms Lives! Read for enjoyment and enlightenment."

"Oh, My Redwood Heart!"

"Oh, My Redwood Heart!"

The Joyful and Heartbreaking Marriage of a Shy Woman and a Schizoaffective Man

Debbie Bumstead

**To Life, to Love,
to Memory, to the Written Word**

❧Contents ❧

Part One

❧First Date ❧
1982 Journal - Selected Entries

Something nice happened to me yesterday afternoon on Valentine's Day. I was at home when Phil, my neighbor in the duplex, appeared at the glass patio door. He and I had been talking to each other a lot lately in passing through the yard. But now he stood without knocking, and I thought it kind of funny. Then I opened the door and he brought out a heart-shaped box of chocolates from behind his back! I said thank you several times and offered him a piece, but he thought he better not, and he went back to his apartment. From my table, I picked up one of the child's valentines I'd let my friend's little girls play with yesterday, and I put "to Phil from Debbie" on the back. On the front the card had a picture of a pig holding a box of candy and saying, "Next to Candy I like you best!" I took the valentine over to Phil and he laughed when he read it.

**

Phil told me he is 39; that's twelve years older than I am, and I had thought he was younger. The truth is, I think I'm a little in love with him, just for being there next door. I hear him come in from his casino job late at night - his car door slams right outside my bedroom window, and then I hear his apartment door scrape shut because it is warped, and I know I'm not alone in the duplex anymore. In the afternoons, as he gets ready for his work, I smell his shaving lotion as it wafts through the thin walls, and then I see him cross the yard, his reddish hair shining brightly like a helmet! For awhile his car was in for repairs, so I let him use my phone and then we visited in my living room while he waited for the taxi to take him to work.

**

We went on a first date last night, but it was also a good-bye date. He told me there's a program in Utah where a person can learn to be a piano tuner, and he wants to enter it. He's been working here and saving up his money a long time and plans to leave in a day or two.

I wore forest green corduroy pants, a pretty sweater, and my beige corduroy jacket. My hair hung down loose. Phil wore his work slacks and a white shirt. Funny thing, he had a similar jacket, but of dark brown. I was stiff with shyness as we got into his car and drove through downtown Reno's flashing lights and busy sidewalks. All the casinos beckoned us in, but we decided to go to Marie Callendar's, where we sat in a booth across from each other, and I hid behind my hair.

The waitress came to ask if we wanted drinks. I shook my head, and Phil said, "You can if you want, Debbie."

"I don't really drink," I replied.

When the waitress left, Phil told me, "I don't like drinking, either; it always makes me a little sick."

Phil continued talking easily about himself, and then he asked me questions. To hear my answers, he bent his head to look up into my down-turned face with his red-brown eyes that match his curly hair. That little movement to catch my eyes endears him to me more than ever. But my mind was observing from a distance, too, and I felt maybe he was talking too much, that something was different about him, that he was going too far compared to how little time we've known each other.

At the theater we watched *Reds*, about an American man in Russia during their Revolution. I felt shy when the sex scenes came on, and I think we both became extra still in our seats. At the Intermission, as we stood in the lobby together, Phil asked me if I wanted to go home. I said I'd like to stay. I was very conscious of my long hair hanging down and keeping me safe.

On the way back home, as we passed through the bright lights again, Phil told me, "I like you. You are sincere."

"I am?" I asked.

"Yes, you are yourself," he said, and I replied, "Well, I like you, too."

We parted on my porch, and he went around to his own place. Now later I'm thinking, maybe what struck me as curious about Phil was the way he revealed himself so soon, telling of his deep thoughts and concerns. I read somewhere that when a person does that to another and the other does not reciprocate, a light barrier is set up unconsciously, and it's as if the first person were a little strange to have revealed himself, even though he may only have been being honest. Then if the relationship continues things usually equal out and so go on the right track again. But Phil is moving away this week sometime and that will be that.

**

This morning Phil left on his trip to Utah. I was up early to go to class at the University, and I noticed him from my window out by our cars. He held a snow brush and gently swished the light snow off the windows of my car. The sight was a moment of hurting love for me - seeing just that gentle swish, his tall figure, his big coat, his manliness, and feeling his thoughtfulness. I hurried out with my notebook on my hip. We stood together fresh face to fresh face and said a few words.

Debbie Bumstead

"What is your major?" he asked.

"I'm getting into the M.A. program in English," I said. "I like to write."

He irritated me a smidgen by replying, "I used to want to be a writer, too." As if my writing would be just a passing whim!

But I smiled. "Thanks for brushing the snow off, but I planned to walk down today."

"Good-bye, Debbie," Phil told me. I felt warm with his pleasant voice saying my name, as if he were touching me in some way.

But "Good-bye," I said, "and good luck in your life."

I walked up the hill to the main street, looked back once, and saw him now softly brushing snow off his own car.

I feel like I've missed knowing him better; I feel like I've missed something special.

❧At Last I Am Tamed ❧
1983 Memories

Easter always reminds me of Phil coming back to Reno from Utah in 1983. He was a changed man, heavier and sadder. Why did he go in the first place? Later on I learned of his propensity to have big ideas, to follow dreams, to travel to distant cities in different states, and then to fail, to become depressed, to return home broken. In this case, he went to learn the trade of piano-tuner at a college there. But he couldn't stick with it; he simply worked as a Pinkerton guard in order to save his money and come back.

It wasn't as if he and I were boyfriend and girlfriend, but I did write him a couple of letters, and he wrote me a couple. In one of my college classes, I read Saul Bellow's *Seize the Day*, and somehow both the story and the cover picture on the paperback reminded me of Phil. Fascinated, as soon as I finished the novel, I reread it twice. But I also daydreamed about another guy in the M.A. program. And I later learned while in Utah, Phil was asking out the waitress at the doughnut shop where he ate breakfast (but she refused, said she was married).

Then he made it back to his family in Fallon, came to Reno again, and rented a room down at my family's motel. Grandmother told me he was back. On Easter she handed me a chocolate bunny he had wanted her to give me. He came over one afternoon to my country corner house next to the motel, and we went somewhere, I can't remember where. I only remember that as we drove, he said he had wanted to kiss me when he saw me, but he was afraid someone at the motel might see.

So when we got back to my house and went into the living room, we stood facing each other, smiling, and then hugged and kissed for the first time. Long afterwards he told me he liked the way I had hugged him, patting him on the back like he was a child. I told him that for me my first romantic kiss made the air around us get a little dark and trembling, like maybe I was going to faint.

***

The Hill House duplex where Phil and I had lived before was now rented out to two other people. I had moved to a smaller cottage on the same acreage of the Wagon Wheel Motel, which was a six room motel run by my mom and my grandparents. It sat on the north side of University land and had been there since the 50s when my grandpa and my dad had built it, and planted the trees, bushes and big lawn, and decorated it all with loose wagon wheels chained to trees, and two or three old west wagons sitting on the grass.

Grandmother and Grandpa Marlow both worked for the "SP" - the Southern Pacific Railroad - from the 1940s and then from the fifties also ran the motel, coming home to clean up rooms and rent them out nightly to travelers. Time went on, my grandparents retired, and they now rented rooms out by the week to mostly casino workers, exclusively men, and some of these men stayed for years. My mom, brothers, and I knew the renters by their room numbers and also by Grandmother's funny stories about them.

Because of Grandmother's funny stories, we knew that

most of the renters were a little eccentric or loners or ill in some way. Before I even met Phil, when I was still living near my dad and his parents and working in California, Grandmother wrote me she had a man for me. That was Phil, who had a toothy "salesman's smile," she said. So Phil knew Grandmother and Grandpa before he knew me; they invited him for lunches down at their motel apartment, and there Phil and Grandmother sometimes discussed the Bible.

I didn't think much about the "man for me" before I met him; maybe he was just another of Grandmother's funny stories, I thought, and she was teasing me. When I met him, though, and fell in love, I thought since he was working two jobs, he was a normal working type of man, poor perhaps, but sturdy and strong. It was only when I got to know him better, I saw that he, also, was troubled in some eccentric way that I couldn't quite describe at first.

I even had a dream one night, halfway through our courtship, that I shouldn't marry him. But how could I ignore love, and, anyway, what would I have become without the cherished struggle of my 25 year career of loving Phil? I liked instead to remember another dream I had soon after we first hugged and kissed. I dreamed I had an apartment on the second floor of a Victorian house that was very nicely decorated with oak floors and good furniture, a large living room, and a bedroom with a big soft bed. Phil was sitting on the bed talking to me. He wore black silk boxer shorts and suspenders to hold them up. I thought his outfit awfully funny; I woke up laughing.

***

Anyone meeting Phil and knowing him casually would consider him a friendly man with intelligence and wisdom, full of kindness and interest in others. He was that man. That was the man who came to me magically, it seemed, to help **my** particular eccentric loneliness! I was so shy I barely spoke up in groups besides my family, and as for men, I had become friends with two or three along the way, but none seemed to see me as a sexual person. Inside I was dying for love, romantic and sexual love.

Phil tamed me just like *The Little Prince* tamed the Fox. I guess like many other people, I can't get over how true that little story is to my life. My heart feels very full when I think of my Phil, my Prince.

One evening soon after his return, we sat in my living room to play a game of chess, and while we played we started getting to know each other. "Were you married before?" he asked me.

"No, I've never been married," I said, and then added, "Grandmother told me you were once."

"Yes, that's all over now," Phil said.

Phil won the chess game. He said, "Whew!" and pretended to mop his forehead.

"What?" I asked, and he said, "I was afraid you would win and I'd look dumb."

I laughed. I realized he thought I was an intellectual, getting an M.A. and reading a lot, and that perhaps inside I was judging his own lack of a college degree. That, however, never crossed my mind. I thought he was stronger than I, more knowledgeable about life, and later when he told me that in the Air Force they had given him an I.Q. test and he was 140 plus, I wasn't surprised. He was a genius!

***

It was true what I'd read about men and women sharing their past romantic histories with each other early on. "I had a girlfriend in Fallon awhile ago, but that ended badly," Phil told me.

His wife, he had married in his early twenties. They broke

8

up, but got back together, but then broke up again for good. "She was the type to get up on desks and dance at office parties," he told me.

Then there was the gal in Alaska he met while camping out, when he traveled around the country on a motorcycle. He liked that she was a mother with a young child, so they got to talking over a picnic table, and he ended up staying in her tent. "It hurts a little to talk of her," he told me, "I think I loved her."

Then had come the gal in Fallon, near Reno, where he lived with his family after his travels. "She was too pretty for me," he said, "and she went crazy mad and rammed her car into mine."

"Why was she so angry?" I asked.

"She was a madhead," Phil said.

He didn't explain any of his break-ups. But I guessed why much later.

***

That summer Phil drove me in his red car east along 80, out of Reno, and into the long desert to go to the town of Fallon. First we passed the low hills along the edge of the Truckee River and by the hamlet of Mustang, which housed the famous brothel, the Mustang Ranch. Here, too, I was once thrilled as Phil told me, "I went there a couple of times when I was desperate."

He was a man! That's what I believed of him, and what stirred my own sexual desires. Gradually, gradually I was tamed by his kisses and hugs. That first visit to Fallon, I didn't meet his parents. They were out, so we sat in their house for awhile; Phil took a seat on the sofa, while I sat on a chair far across the room. He patted the cushion beside him, and when I bashfully took my place, he put his arm around me, his hand on my hip. How stiff I was with shyness! The touch was what I craved, yet how frightened I was. And how kind Phil was, so slow and undemanding. We just sat and talked, and bit by bit my muscles relaxed. And the next time we sat together was easier.

I was like a wild filly, unused to humans, and Phil was like the horse whisperer - soothing me, gentling me by touch.

***

Finally I met Phil's parents. "My mom is kind of nervous," Phil warned me. But I loved Doris from the moment we met; she was tall, with dark red-brown hair and eyes like Phil's, and a tomboyish manner despite her nervous arm movements and talkativeness. She had grown up on a farm in Montana. Phil's dad was not my favorite person; he was rough and critical towards Phil, I thought. But Doris's encompassing love had saved all her children from their rough dad, and I saw Phil warmly embraced by the rest of the family, and I was, as well, as I eventually met them all, his older brother, his younger sister, and the youngest brother and all their spouses and children. Each family had its own furniture store now, in this or that place, a tradition started by the father.

Phil's family gave him odd jobs that summer - one was tearing down an old shack on his grandma's property. Here, Phil told me of a neighbor's dog, Buddy, a little Boston Terrier, who tried to pick up a two by four as a stick to play with him. Laughing at Buddy's brave move led to getting our own Boston years later.

The second job was doing "the Box Pile" at the furniture store. Phil would back the furniture van up to a fenced-in square where all the big cardboard boxes were thrown after unpacking the chairs and sofas. Then both of us threw and trampled boxes into the truck. Being with Phil, doing something I'd never done before I felt full of fun, and Phil was laughing and happy, too, as we worked. I felt fine as we got into the cab and Phil drove way out to the Fallon dump, where we reversed our actions. Despite the smell, the long views of hilly garbage, and the white seagulls swirling above like flies, I loved it. And when we finished our job and drove home to Reno again in Phil's sporty car at dusk, I loved passing the wide wild desert and the roadside pools that reflected the pinky turquoise sky like jewels.

***

I had no history to tell Phil, really, because I had no sexual experience with boyfriends. I had wounds from an evil uncle far in the past before I was six that had seared into me the fear I lived with, and I couldn't talk to Phil about it yet. But, after all, I had to share something. So I told him about the boyfriend I'd had in high school and college, but not that the boy had never even held my hand. That kind boy had been safe for me, but in the end I wanted to grow, so I had left him behind. For six years now I'd been alone.

Then I thought I might lose Phil, too, one strange afternoon when we went to the Reno Keystone Theater. Unique or old movies were shown there, and we went to see Hitchcock's *Rear Window*. In the lobby before the movie, a lot of people milled around, and one of them, a mature-looking woman in a bright shift, touched Phil's shoulder and asked, "Phil?"

"Oh!" Phil exclaimed. "Lucy, I haven't seen you in years!" I could see Phil's face blushing, his manner all embarrassed and blunder-y. They chatted a moment. Then she looked at me, and Phil turned. He couldn't remember my name to introduce me.

"I'm Debbie," I said.

"Oh, I'm sorry," Phil said to me, and the woman laughed and tried to smooth my feathers.

"I always loved the way Phil's eyes matched his hair,"

Lucy remarked as we stood there. "You've put on some weight, I see," she said to Phil, poking his stomach.

This little banter didn't soothe me at all. I was already sad behind my smiling face.

Lucy was with her mother, and both women seemed to me a little drunk. We visited a bit more, and Lucy gave Phil her phone number. "Let's get together and talk over old times," she said to him. Then she and her mom went into the movie in front of us, and Phil and I sat behind them a ways up, so that we were far enough apart to be private.

"Was she a girlfriend?" I whispered to Phil, and "Yes," he whispered back, "in high school, and then I met her again about ten years ago." As the movie played I sometimes looked over, spying on Lucy as James Stewart spied on his murderous neighbor. Forever afterwards that movie stayed vivid in my mind, and at the time, I wrote a poem for my poetry class to describe my feelings:

Rear Window
We went to see the Hitchcock film
And you met an old girlfriend in the lobby.
I stood alongside while you talked,
For a minute you forgot my name - I
Had to tell her I was Debbie.
During the movie I sat with you
And she sat over there with her old mom;
While Jimmy and Grace watched their neighbor,
I watched her. Ten years ago you knew her;
Before that you had a wife; after that you had
Others. The way you bent down to reassure me
In the dark of the show, it doesn't seem
Like you should have such a big past behind you -
I hate looking out that rear window.

After the movie, as we were driving home, I asked Phil if

he planned to call her and see her. "I probably will," he said, and I fell silent.

Then I said aloud my heart's hurt, "I guess that's the end of me!"

Phil burst out with a laugh, until he looked over and saw I was unhappy. "No it isn't, Debbie," he reassured me. "I'm with you now. We are going to be married one day."

"Oh," I said, smiling.

"I just ran into her a few years ago once, and before then, she was a high school girlfriend," he told me again. But then he did add the detail that she was his "first time," which didn't help my jealous heart.

He went to eat with Lucy not long after, but it was just one lunch and a good-bye. But long after, through the years, sometimes Phil brought the incident up, how I'd said, "I guess that's the end of me!" Then he'd laugh and squeeze me.

***

Finally, as the summer came to a close, one evening Phil and I sat talking, and I told him, "I've never had anyone make love to me."

"Oh!" He was surprised. Well, I was in my late 20s, I had the look of a casual hippy girl, and I wasn't religious like my Grandmother or his own family. Anyone would assume I was experienced; at least, I hoped so, for this was a secret I'd never told anyone before.

Then I asked Phil, "Would you make love to me?"

Phil laughed with embarrassment, as if I were teasing, but I was serious. I mean, I was easy with him now, could sit with him, be kissed by him; I loved holding hands as we walked, bumping into him for fun, and even smoothing his red curls back with my fingers. I wanted to be free of the last fear; I so wanted to be free of the dark past which had purpled my natural desires with so much horror, that I'd never let a regular fellow close before! But with Phil's taming, I was ready now; I could overcome the fear of intercourse, I thought.

"I was hoping we'd get married first," Phil said slowly, "but I know how you feel." He got up and came to sit near me. He put his arm around me and whispered, "When we are married, we'll do wicked things."

"I don't want to wait," I said. We looked at each other, smiled at each other.

"Maybe in a day or two," Phil said. "I have to think."

"OK." I was happy. It would happen.

A day or two later Phil came over to spend the night. We watched a little TV and had a snack. Phil told me he had had a bit of backache today, and I said, "Oh, ok." That must have taken the pressure off, for he soon asked me to come sit on his lap. Awkwardly I sat on his sturdy knees and hugged him, trying to relax.

When we undressed for bed, we lay all pleasantly naked beside each other. "I haven't been with a woman in a long time," Phil told me. He turned to me and nuzzled his head to my breasts, and so it went on. Afterwards, I was glad, and ready for the next time.

❧A Hundred Inventions ❧
1984 - Memories

Phil couldn't keep a job long. He excelled in interviews. I counted up all the jobs he had gotten in Reno in just one year; it was something like 34! He was just so personable and good natured; everybody liked him. But as soon as the position began, somehow his spirits plummeted, and he quit within a few days or weeks. A casino vault man job, though, seemed to suit him for awhile. After my own day of work as Teacher's Aide in a first grade, I used to peek through my kitchen window curtains at night to see if Phil's room light was on. Then I knew he was up and getting ready to go on the night shift.

I tapped on his door, quietly, as Grandmother's apartment was close. I used to laugh to myself, meanly, as Phil and I lay naked together on his bed - Grandmother didn't know what I was up to! Then I would sit watching Phil iron his slacks, his slow hands I loved so much pushing the iron back and forth on the board, as he stood in his underwear and smiled at me.

***

Like Phil, I wasn't that great at work, either. I used to daydream I'd be a professional, like a veterinarian, an oceanographer, or a child psychologist. But I had taken up writing in kindergarten; from then on, it was all I wanted to do, to write books like the ones I so loved to read. At the time then, when I was 30, I had finished a novel that my mentors thought good, and that an agent had accepted to send out.

Phil's vocation was invention. His mind was prolific with ideas. The first I was introduced to was a very simple idea for a Cup Cupboard or a Cup Safe. "I worked in an office once," Phil told me, "and in the kitchen everyone had their coffee mugs on a shelf all hodgepodge, and sometimes other people used other people's cups. So my idea is for a decorated wooden or acrylic box to keep the mug safe." Phil thought I was pretty good at drawing, so he suggested, "Maybe you can do some decorations for the cup cupboards. I thought one might look like a safe with a painted dial, or another with the words Cup Cupboard in fancy design."

I liked Cup Cupboards; the wooden box my brother made and the acrylic one Phil ordered at a plastics place did seem nifty and useful, as we tried out different mugs in them. But how was Phil to get the money to make a bunch, or market them, or sell them? That always broke him down. While his big mind went far ahead, into many stores, all over the country, making millions, buying a house for us, and making us rich, the Cup Cupboards got dusty, and we finally put them away.

Phil had an idea for a game called Make Tracks! that had to do with matching animal tracks to their sources. I crafted a homespun-looking wooden board with cards and tokens; we tested it on a child we knew, and it was fun. I thought we could make the boards ourselves, sell them small, like in craft fairs, but Phil's mind was much bigger. It was make it rich, or nothing, and Make Tracks! also fell by the wayside.

Phil's biggest most precious idea he called The Interpreter. The Interpreter was like a religion to him, something that would revolutionize the world, for it was a universal language, which anyone with any language would understand. Words would become pictures. Phil had pages of explanations, and when I read them, it seemed as if it were really an intelligent idea. But at the same time, I could not figure it out at all. In Phil's beautiful mind, the idea encompassed the world and even had emotional feelings running through it, mostly about remorse - remorse in the Interpreter had deep meaning for Phil. I wasn't able to comprehend it, though, and he was not able to sift out a reasonable description to go on with it, in the real world.

Time went on: I wrote many books, stories, and poems, and Phil thought up a hundred inventions. Each one of our ideas was a baby born to be loved, and each one sparkled for a moment and flitted away. I ended up with pages, reams, of writings - it was sad the way my writing never succeeded to the extent I and others had believed it could, but by then I couldn't stop it. And Phil ended up with a list of as many as I could remember of his inventions, on a page in his funeral book. The inventions marked with asterisks were ones which I discovered were invented sometime later, so I knew they would have worked, if only we had had the money, the knowledge, the contacts. I don't know why else our struggle to be special was so ridden with failure. Unless we tried our best, and it wasn't good enough.

***

Phil's spirit for work crumbled again, and his parents helped him to apply for Social Security Disability. I found out that in that great big past of his, before we had ever met, he had been on SSD before. He had been diagnosed at the Veteran's Hospital as mentally ill with terms like ADHD and Manic-Depressive in his chart.

He told me that after his divorce once, he had been stopped by police for driving the wrong way on a street in San Francisco, and when he got out of the car, he talked gibberish. They took him to a mental hospital where he said they gave him drugs and he felt like he was dead. This story gave me pause, but even it didn't make a difference; he was still Phil to me, and I loved him.

In 1984 his parents set Phil up in a modern clean apartment in Carson City to help him start again with a new outlook. He still wanted to marry me, but his great worry was not being able to make a living. Well, I thought, I had fallen in love with him for being such a good worker at first, but it wasn't that important to me. I came from a long line of males who couldn't make much of a living because they chose the creative side of their souls - my grandpa Bumstead, my dad, my brothers. And I was like that, too, though I now had a part-time job as a Teaching Assistant at the community college that I stuck with a long time.

But Phil's family members were all hard workers, business people, doing well. Phil felt like the black sheep. As the years passed, I found out it was Phil's overriding concern that obsessed him constantly: how to work and make money, in order to be his own definition of a man. He never ever gave up or relaxed his pursuit, not even after his first near brush with death.

❦Together We Travel ❦
1985 - Memories

On January 3 I drove down to Carson City to stay with Phil in his apartment. At home I had told Grandmother and Mama that Phil and I were getting married tomorrow.

"Are you sure?" Mama asked. She liked Phil, but probably saw the trouble ahead; after all my dad had been of a similar design to Phil - the dreamer type they were called in her generation - and that had been hard.

"Yes," I said, irritably, and Mama was quiet.

Grandmother congratulated me, though. Maybe she thought it a good idea, considering he and I had been "engaged" for a couple of years.

Later that day Phil and I sat in a Carson City restaurant, drinking coffee and hot cocoa, holding hands, making plans. Phil took his ever present pen from his breast pocket and scribbled on a napkin:

Little Flower
AGAIN AND
AGAIN I
Love you
More

And that evening before our marriage, we two sat comfortably on his couch and watched a program on TV. Phil had his arm around my shoulder, his right hand hanging down, when he suddenly used a finger to circle around my nipple through my shirt. Ah! Instant response. I turned my face to him, and we smiled.

***

January 4, 1985 we went to the Justice of the Peace in Carson City. Phil wore a nice shirt and slacks, and a gray cardigan; I wore an outfit he had chosen for me, a wool skirt, blouse, and cardigan, too. We looked at each other and laughed, saying like ever after whenever we tried to dress up, "Here we are, ready for the Ugly Bug Ball."

We were just so plain and unmade-up. A person had to know us, really look at us, to see any beauty. I thought Phil handsome because of his wonderful eyes and hair, his straight nose, his tall broad-shouldered body. I didn't count his weight, his round chin, his large head like other people might have. On the other hand, Phil had a poorer opinion of my looks, and I can remember several comments that hurt me.

Such as: "When I first met you, I decided looks didn't matter as much as in the past." Or, if I asked if I was as pretty as this or that person, he would think not, I could tell by his smile. "You are the one for me, pretty or plain," he'd say. But he pleased me often, called my eyes dark blue-gray, instead of just blue, and he told me I had a nice profile, and my hair smelled good. He liked the way I put my hair up in back on hot days, that was one of the things he first noticed about me, as I worked in the yard at the duplex before we spoke. Later he called me beautiful one evening as I stood in the doorway of the bedroom, dressed in silky pjs. That was early on when I was slim. When I was heavy in middle age, I stood undressing in our bedroom, and saw him looking at me, and I apologized for getting fat. He replied, "Don't think of that. I don't see your fat; I just see you are a woman." That was so wise and true, and exactly how I had looked on him earlier when he had that big "milk belly" from drinking a gallon of the white stuff every day.

So there we stood in front of the judge for our ceremony, the secretary witnessed, and we shyly kissed afterwards. We drove to Lake Tahoe for a meal out, and the day ended sadly back in Phil's apartment. Sadly, because I thought we would have a night of lovemaking, like all the movies showed and books described. We'd made love the night before, but Phil wasn't in the mood now. And that was when I began to learn about that.

***

"I wish you were a Christian," Phil had said to me once, when we were courting. Then he told me, "I saw an angel once. It was my Grandpa John, and he was this big." He indicated about an inch with his fingers.

He was serious. I knew lots of people liked to believe in angels and other kooky-to-me ideas. Even educated, wise, intelligent men and women believed in God, so I figured faith was something people needed sometimes. But sometimes the belief was trouble, in the world, and in my Phil.

I'd read the Bible twice in the past, but found I didn't like God very much in the old stories. I wanted to believe in an afterlife, too, but discovered that was impossible for me, too much of a daydream, even after trying a long time. When I finally gave up the effort to have faith, my spirit bloomed freely, all pretty and wide and blue sky. At last I didn't have to be disappointed in God for what happened in the world, or guilty within myself for the bad things that happened to me. At last the world was as it was! How wonderful that unanswered prayers no longer were the fault of the not-faithful-enough person who prayed! How beautiful now my life, my one and only, to treasure and build as best I could! I could still be kind, of course, and my deepest need to tell the truth and live as a good person didn't have to rely on faith in an afterlife. I was glad; my release from the heaviness of religion truly freed me.

Phil understood. Very often, he would say, "I feel that way, too." But, that was when he felt well. When his illness dipped into the dark area of his brain, the Bible, God, and Jesus became twisted in with rules, sins, even prejudices, and sometimes hallucinations. I knew this many years later. In our first year of marriage, I just didn't understand.

"You will understand some day," he'd tell me, when I begged for love, and he'd refuse. "We can be together sexually," he'd try to explain, "without really doing that. And one day we will want a child; then we'll be together."

Oh, oh, I'd cry furiously. I'd rush into the bedroom to throw myself onto the bed, sobbing. What had happened to my loving physical man with the gentle hands and manly body? I'd never been able to show my anger to anyone, but with Phil I felt free to be furious; that was the only good thing about it.

"I'm sorry, Debbie, I know how you feel," Phil said, sitting by me on the bed. "I had that need, too, when I was young." He told about his first wife, who was extra sexual, I guess, with experience of more than just the something simple I wanted. "It was too much for me," he said. "It was like making love became just fucking. It was not God's way."

Now I guessed why his first wife and girlfriends had left him in anger; he'd probably stopped wanting to make love to them, too. That first year was almost too hard for me, but sometimes the good Phil came out again, and we made love; one day we made love twice! I kept count that year, and we got together 17 times.

The next year was better; he eased up, and we made a deal that we'd make love once a week. That was enough for me, so my fury subsided, and we began to be content. I was sorry sex had to be so important to me, for Phil's sake, but without sex, I got a weird and scary panicky feeling, like I was going back to being only attractive to sexless safe men, like my former boyfriend. I couldn't go back to that past where I unconsciously tried to protect myself from the pedophile uncle of my childhood. I needed to blast that evil man away with real love!

***

One April morning Phil and I left the animals, Rex, Holly, Monty and Pie under Mama's care at the cottage where we now lived together across from the motel. We drove away in our orange Fiesta, north, to visit Red Bluff, California, Phil's hometown. A long stretch of north country led along the valley between Reno and Susanville, with lots of small towns and lakes and bluffs. In Susanville we stopped for coffee. I loved the early morning, the feeling of a road trip, all the impressions that made up such trips, like the hisses and rumblings of semi-trucks, the passing scenery, glimpses of life in action and then gone, the constant cars, each one filled with at least one brain thinking all sorts of big thoughts of life. Then the coffee shop cafes and the waitresses, the sleepy need for a sugary snack, and the restrooms - a whole poem's worth of essences made up the road trips Phil and I took through our marriage.

Together We Travel
The road curves, rushing through the past –
Our little car like a jolt of memory
Zips up and down, around and around --
Oh, the trips we took, the journeys we planned,
The paths we followed, the years we traveled.
Forests of flickering light and shadow,

Debbie Bumstead

How many forests we sped through
Like a swooping bird, and every time,
Every time, glances, smiles, loving together
The limitless beauty of the trees.
Oh, all the stops at mini-marts and cafes,
All the food we ate, all the restrooms we visited!
All the people we saw, speaking to some,
Watching others without a word,
Everywhere we went, children playing
Women talking, men laughing,
Every single one an individual
With a whole life's trip bundled up inside
Like a treasure map -- they are all out there now
Somewhere in the world we once traveled.

Remember the motels, the cool clean rooms
Folding around us the quiet of rest,
And all the times we made love in strange beds,
Far away from home, each encounter
Like some exciting best-loved and well-known
Journey within a journey. Then --
Mornings, extra bright with sometimes sun,
Sometimes snow, and you'd say,
"The weather is a character,"
And we'd drive onward, explorers
Discovering our own bit of earth,
While within, on the map of memories,
We marked each turn, each curve,
Each mountain, each valley,
Each red-pinned point of interest.
Remember? We smoothed out all the map's
Rumpled creases using our loving hearts;
With our hands clasped and a light kiss,
We shared smiles for the infinite journey.

After Susanville, on this April, 1985 that we were calling a honeymoon, we then turned into the manzanita-covered hills that led into the Plumas mountains, the pine forests. We stopped at Guernsey Camp that was famous in Phil's family - here they had gathered with other relatives during summers to spend weeks at a time in tents or cabins beside a small stream in the woods. Childhood memories were poignant for Phil, as if they showed a little world of purity and delight that later disappeared as he grew older. I loved listening to his stories of cooking on the fire, of catching fish, of lots and lots of cousins and siblings playing together.

When we came down the other side into Red Bluff, I saw spring was well on its way, not so measly as it was in Reno yet. The trees were green or blossoming as they lined the small town streets, and the lawns were crisp in front of the old style houses.

"This was ours," Phil said, stopping the car in front of a modest house in an old neighborhood. And I imagined him there as a bitty red-headed boy with his baby Easter duck he loved so much. How moving was his memory of how the duck grew up into a big white bird, and his Dad gave it to a farmer, and Phil, in his bed that night, thought he could hear his duck calling to him through the window.

We ate lunch in a Diner with a Jukebox that had table top extensions, so we could order a couple of old songs while we waited for our meal. Phil pointed across the street at the building where his dad, his Grandpa Fred, and Uncle Glenn had had an auto parts store.

"Sometimes I went with them on deliveries all over the area," Phil told me. His Grandpa Fred wasn't his dad's father, but his mom's and Uncle Glenn was her brother. Uncle Glenn and another brother, Uncle Bill were in many more fond memories than Phil's dad, I noticed, and when I met Glenn, I, too, was impressed with how kind he was. Uncle Bill was often talked about by the whole family, but he had committed suicide not too long ago.

I liked to imagine Phil playing with his big brother, his small sister and brother, and all the girl cousins whose names began with J there in Red Bluff or other towns they moved to in the vicinity. One of these J cousins sent me a sympathy card after Phil died, describing young Phil as "our golden boy" because he was so gentle, talkative, fun, and full of ideas.

When Phil and I drove out of Red Bluff, up the hills into the mountains again, I was filled with so much joy that I noticed it and noticed it, seeing how beautiful it was to be happy! I think mostly the happiness was the realization of love. Phil and I loved each other. I can't describe to someone who isn't extremely shy, the total relief and freedom that came to me with the love of Phil. Here at last was the "pardner" I'd wanted when playing cowboy as a kid, the secret lover I'd wanted through puberty, and the seemingly unattainable goal of connection I'd wanted in the lonely years of my 20s.

***

In Reno we often drove around, too. Maybe we'd go out by the southern neighborhood to cruise the winding streets of high-priced homes, all built too close together with lots of gables and towers and xeroscaping. Phil said we'd live there when his business succeeded. We cruised down further south of Reno into the farm area where owners had green land, trees, horses. That was more my style. To the west of town a secret dirt road we knew in the little town of Verdi led us to a small creek where we let Rex and Holly run and play. There we experienced the way the wind came down from the mountains - first we'd hear it in the pines a distance away, then we'd see it coming closer as it stirred the trees just west of us, and finally all around in the needles of the trees above us, the wind rustled strongly, singing and wafting pine perfume.

"Oh, My Redwood Heart!"

Phil had camped out as a child, but I had not. He wanted to show me how fun it was, so that first summer we bought a blue pup tent, stocked up on food, and drove west to Donner Lake. Phil cooked dinner on the charcoal grill, and we toasted marshmallows. The trees surrounded us, their thin trunks bare until high up the foliage spread out, and mountain jays came to speak to us. That night in the tiny pup tent, we spread the sleeping bag and blankets out into a bed on the thin air mattress. I couldn't get to sleep at all. Tossing, turning, I grew more and more irritated, until Phil said, "Come here close." I snuggled into his body, spooning, and he held me so tight, I couldn't move. Then I slept.

☆San Diego Magic & Sun Rise Star ☆
1986 - Memories

How did I explain it to myself, I wonder. In the first two years of marriage, Phil lived away from me at least ten times. He tried Carson City, San Francisco, Lake Tahoe, Kalispel in Montana, Seattle, Medford, Oregon, and Sacramento. My thoughts as he left were always - why did he have to be apart from me? What was inside his mind that convinced him somewhere else would work? Without knowing the words to explain his problem, though, I think I understood as people do when they have to withstand something inevitable. And - he always came back to me within days or a couple of weeks or a month.

Love made it easy for me to get over a separation or even a daily fuss. If my feelings were hurt, Phil had only to hold out his arm to me from his seat, or to hug me in the middle of the kitchen, or to come sit on the bed while I cried, for me to let it go. We both used a code phrase when an argument was getting too hot - the line from a 60s song, "Don't hurt me now.." with a smile to soften anger.

I think I learned from Phil to let go of little things. Very early on, one day we were stopping at a 7/11 store for Phil to get a treat, when I righteously reminded him that he was trying to lose weight (this was when he was big and I was thin), and Phil replied, "If a couple isn't careful, a whole marriage can be ruined by little jabs at each other like that." He said this thoughtfully, kindly, and I took it to heart. I have remembered his words since then and still tell this story sometimes to friends, as if maybe I could teach them as Phil taught me.

Love is great in size, I found with Phil, so great it surrounds everything, and yet love lets go just as much as it surrounds. It is interesting to me that the Greek root word "Phil" means love. I could say that Loving Phil meant also Loving Love.

***

A ground floor room with an outside access in a big Victorian house near Balboa Park in San Diego - chance brought us to this treasure-like interval in our second summer of marriage. San Diego, Phil had considered back in Reno, might be the place for him, where he might succeed finally. Since I wanted to go to Hemet to see my friends and relatives, I could take him the 80 miles south to drop him in the city.

As we drove into downtown on the freeway, I saw the greenery of San Diego crowding down to the very edges of the pavement and even over the sides of the overpass bridges, and it gave me the oddest feeling of being in the past. Time traveling back to 1972-76 when I went to college here and wandered with friends, or maybe even further back to 1964-66, when our dad had his handmade trimeran, the *Magic*, moored at Shelter Island and we came for sailing weekends, all the family.

"Let's get a paper, and look for a room," Phil said, excited, too. We stood together in a phone booth, studying the fine print of the newspaper. The first place we called invited us over and we took it, a studio in a lovely old Victorian house. We bought a bed at a thrift store, and somehow in all the excitement, I decided to stay. It was the first time I went and stayed with Phil on one of his escapes.

The landlord, who lived in the rest of the house, was a

young man who had a pet tortoise that tumbled about in the lumpy grass of the backyard. Another neighbor walked by each day, a huge bear-man with two floppity Pekinese on leashes bobbing in front of him. Many of the houses had bars on the windows, and though there was a fine mansion at the end of our street, the whole neighborhood was not the best place to live. I believe our studio was occupied by a drug dealer before we came along, because for a couple of weeks, we had many night knockers that we had to turn away, telling them that guy doesn't live here anymore.

Our room had a plate glass window completely covered on the outside by a camellia bush, so it looked like a pretty painting of leaves and sunshine on the wall. We had a table and two chairs, the bed, a minute kitchen, and a bathroom with a tub in which cockroaches wearily crawled around until they entered the deadly Roach Motel I hated putting down.

Phil and I were on our own; I was happy, but it felt scary, too, knowing as we fiddled about with our lives, many thousands were living theirs so near to us. Phil kept to his promise; we made love each week. One day I ran into the landlord in the yard, and seeing his sharp glance at me, I realized that since his bedroom was above ours, he'd probably heard us. I had hated in my past the occasions when I heard lovers together, and I felt embarrassed. Strange that though I hated to hear other people making love, yet when I was making the sounds myself, they seemed quite natural.

There were so many San Diego impressions:

Taking walks in the neighborhood with Phil, on beautiful blue sky ocean air days and drinking in and in the lush gardens bundling around the old Victorians, Spanish styles, and mansions we passed.

Our explorations to Balboa Park on lively weekends, all the eucalyptus trees growing like friendly giants with long beards and spotted skins making artist-pleasing scenes of shade, the man on the building-high stilts, the ice cream cones under the fig tree and watching children play.

A drive to Shelter Island, showing Phil the little half moon bay of sand that cousin Donna and I had played on when the *Magic* was in its mooring, and that my boyfriend and I had picnicked on ten years later, and now here was Phil, my husband, standing on the same bright sand and walking back with me over the hump-backed bridge to the parking lot.

That day we also drove up Point Loma to cruise around the campus of what used to be my college and then went down on the other side to the cliffs above the ocean to watch the sunset.

We did well - for awhile. Phil got a guard job downtown, and I commuted to a loan company where I microfilmed properties into a machine. We daydreamed of getting a regular apartment nearer to my job, which promised to become permanent. I made a new friend and visited with old friends; everything was fine. But one day without warning Phil came to my workplace and asked to see me. I went outside with him, and he said, "I have to get away, Debbie. I can't stay here anymore. We have to leave San Diego." He was anxious and desperate; my heart went out to him.

"Can you wait until I finish up at work today?" I asked.

"I can't wait," he said.

Within a couple of hours, we had the car packed with what little we had brought, and we were driving north out of the beauty of San Diego. How well I remember stopping at Red Hawk Hill in Hemet where my dad was living in the cabin, and Phil and I took the little trailer next door for overnight. We snuggled up on the twin bed, and Phil cried.

***

I can count on one hand the times I saw Phil cry in the way I cried almost daily. I felt like I could withstand my crying, but I didn't know if Phil could withstand his. During most of his down times, instead of shedding tears, he took to the bedroom and liked the curtains drawn. He slept during the day and was up all night drawing or writing down his ideas. He drank cups and cups of coffee half filled with milk and sugar. Sometimes, even most times, he liked me coming in to talk to him, or rub his head or lie down beside him, but sometimes he told me, "I want to be alone," and I'd go away.

After we got back to Reno, Phil was so downhearted, he wanted to go stay with his parents in Oregon. Maybe his mother meant safety to him, so that he could be dependent without his big worry of making money and being a man. Meanwhile I stayed alone, alone in our little cottage, with all my family on the Wagon Wheel acreage around me, but no Phil to be free with beside me. I worked at the University and also got a part-time job at a telegraph company. I paid a big telephone bill at the end of the month, from talking to Phil on the phone everyday.

But I wasn't through trying to find an answer. Maybe Phil didn't like being so close to my family; maybe he wanted to be independent of them. I talked on the phone with him about renting an apartment somewhere else here in Reno, and he seemed to perk up. He came back to help me look, and soon we were established in a rented condo, a second-floor almost-new one-bedroom home where we could have our animals.

It was good! For several months we were almost like a normal couple - only better! How beautiful to be together like we were then! How strongly in this moment my heart reaches and reaches for that time of love and joy. I can almost feel Phil's warm shoulder against mine as we sat on the loveseat to talk or watch a TV program, the cats on our laps, and Holly shaking her toy on the floor. We made love every week. When I heard the neighbor woman below us having sex with a boyfriend, I wasn't jealous! She probably heard us, too, as I remember her giving us that sharp glance one time when we met outside our doors. I imagined her thinking we were cute, an old ugly bug couple so in love; ha, I imagined her laughing.

And so we were.

Phil got a guard job, swing shift, and stayed with it awhile. He'd come out from getting dressed in a brown uniform with golden security patches on the shoulders of a big puffy nylon coat, and I'd laugh and hug him. When I saw him like that, so strong and well, I thought of us having a child, and then imagined the little son or daughter looking up at him in his uniform and loving Daddy.

We wanted a child, but we also both had common sense and knew we probably shouldn't - yet, at least. But one day very soon after we had moved into the condo, I collapsed in the kitchen from achy joints and muscles. When I went to the doctor, he said he bet I was pregnant. But in the end I wasn't; instead it was the beginning of fibromyalgia. Not really the beginning, as I'd had freezing up muscles as far back as my first year in Reno, and in San Diego when I played tennis with friends a belt of pain had wrapped around my back.

Fibromyalgia had connotations of being "in your mind" and back then I felt like it was looked on as a sort of way to get out of doing things. I felt like it didn't seem real to some of the people around me. I myself wondered how much I was to blame for my pain - was it the stress of dealing with Phil? But it began before I met him. I was 32 years old, still slim and active, but this disease broke me. The only sweet thing about all the pain and aches of fibromyalgia for me was that Phil knew it was true. He believed in it even more than I did, and showed his concern and care daily. Oh, my, what a sweet man he was about other people's troubles; he was so wise about emotions and failures and the sad truth about life!

So, there I was home alone in the evenings while he worked, and sometimes I put my ear to the wall and listened to the neighbor to our east talk to her visitors. Snoopy! I was writing something, of course, but still not getting published. How I wish now Phil had had an urge to write, rather than invent. The few pieces I have are so fresh and yet slightly

33

unusual, that I think he might have succeeded where I didn't.
I have two poems he wrote during this year at the condo, one
about sunrise and one about sunset.

-- Sun Rise Star --
Birds enter the light and perform --
for children who are there listening --
watching huge wings unfold --
now the sky is changing from
purple and gray -- pink replaces
these skies
And in a little while watchers
must admit that these things
they see
have never happened before

5:l5PM 8-27 Wednesday
Telegram to Debbie
The sky is gray and silver
Shields coming out of the sun
Rain a rare and lingering sight
Sun Down's a moment now
Blue spotted large beige sky
Remains behind the sun light
Leaving a tale of so many
Colors to decide -- while
My heart at last remembering --
The day fades away

❧Phil's Own Words ❧

One Christmas Phil received a big envelope that had some childhood papers and photos of Phil's past that Phil's older brother had found while going through his own keepsakes. I remember my delight in opening the envelope to find the ephemera of Phil's past. I just could not help loving who Phil was as a boy - from the photos of babyhood through his Air Force days, from his mom's words in a baby book, and from his Sunday School certificates and colored pages. When I pulled out Phil's Autobiography written when he was only twelve, Phil and I sat on the couch to read it, and it filled me with joy and love.

My Autobiography
By Philip Winans
April 28, 1955

It was a miserable night so, my mommy says. My dady paced the floor. A while later, he stopped pacing, I had just come into the world, Oct 26, 1942 in Red Bluff, California. I guess my dady was glad to see me because he was so nervous he almost dropped me on the floor. I did not no wether Id like my new dady or not. Soon afterwards, I learned to trust him. For I could tell he loved me. When I had an accident, he always left the room. I suppose he did not want to stick me with a pin.

Two years followed. I took my first two steps, then six

and eight. Finally I was trying my best to walk, any way, I thought my best. My daddy had different ideas. I had just taken twelve struggling steps to walk all the way to my daddy. He kept backing up. So, I stopped, turned around, walked back to where I was and sat down. My daddy was not very proud of me, but at least I was. I learned to turn around.

One year later my dady and I were on the way to the barber shop. A lady walked up to us and said, "What a cute little girl you have." So, naturally, I had a few feelings, too. I just could not wait to get that hair, that made me look like a girl, cut off. It came off. I looked at my dady and mommy, and then, in the mirror and said, "Funny! Funny!" It impressed my parents, so, I thought I better say, "Funny!" more often. So, I said it agin, "Funny, funny!" but this time they were not so impressed. So, I thought I better think up something different to say.

Another year followed, then another. At last I could go to school. The first morning, I just could not wait to get to school. I went, but no one played with me. I wanted to play with the hammer. Another boy walked up and took it away. Naturally, I wanted to stand up for my rights. So, I started to take the hammer back. He hit me on the head with it. I let him have the hammer, and went to look for a good friend. Suddenly I spotted a good friend. She was a girl. I asked her what her name was. She told me, and we became good friends. I still do not no why, that boy hit me with the hammer.

I talked to my teacher frequently. We became very good friends. Her name was Mrs. Marton.

The next year, I had a teacher whoes name was Mrs. Gurnsy. I thought I was pretty big, that year, but I soon learned, that I had a long way to be at the top of the class. One day, Mrs. Gurnsy was reading a story to the class. Suddenly she sneezed, and across the room flew a set of shiney teeth. Everyone started to say, "Mrs. Gurnsy, you dropped your teeth." The class did not know what to think. I started yelling, "False teeth, those are false teeth!" She had to leave us, and we had a new teacher. Her name was Miss Jillson. I was very unhappy to see Mrs. Gurnsy go.

The next year, I had a teacher whoes name was Mrs. Fokerson. She was very nice and kind. The whole class liked her. One thing happened in particular that year. The school was robbed.

The burglar entered through a window at night. He stepped on our clay ceramics. My teachers desk was a mess. The police were there all day. I could not do much work. They were getting fingerprints. It was interesting to watch. The year went by very quickly. I seemed to have every thing finished on time. I received good report card grades.

The next year I was to be in the fourth grade. On the first day of school I was very frightened. My teacher's name was Miss O'Brien. She was my best teacher so far. I liked her very much. She always helped me in my studies. I was doing well in my work. I remember the day I brought a paper to her and said, "Here's my paper, teacher. I am all finished." Miss O'Brien replied, "That is good, Philip, but you must do the other side if I am going to put it on the wall." I said, "Why? Only one side will be showing." I did not mean to be smarty about it. My teacher and a parent laughed and laughed. I did the other side however. Yes, I thought Miss O'Brien was a very nice teacher. I favored her more than any other teacher at the time. I like all my other teachers. I had to leave to go into another room at the end of the year. The name of my school was Lottie Grunsky.

The next teacher I had was Miss Brown. She was as kind as my last teacher. She also helped me very much. I did well, made good grades, and good progress. I read many books that year, and learned much about American history.

One reason I read so much was because my room was in the library. Another, I love to read. Near the end of the year, we went on a swimming party. I had much fun, until I dived too deeply and cut my head. That was all the fun I had that day. Like all bad things, good things have to come to an end. The end of the year came too rapidly, not knowing what was in store for me the next year.

I started school agin in the sixth grade. The first day went smoothly, and quickly for me. I had a teacher whoes name was Mr. Gluth. As the days followed his pleasant shining face seemed to grow grimmer and grimmer.

He corrected the papers only when necessary. He treated most of us very cruelly. The girls mothers were calling all the time, with no result.

The year just dragged. The only time he corrected papers, himself was when he had to, and that wasn't very often. The sixth grade, finally, came to an end, and for the first time in my life I was glad it was over.

When I reached home that afternoon, I was amazed to see a moving van at our house. My mother told me, that we were moving to Marysville. I hated to leave my friends, but I was glad to leave Stockton. Every summer the peat dust would blow, and the town of Stockton was a bit dirty.

When we reached Marysville, I was very happy to see it. I went swimming the first afternoon.

When I first started to school there, I was a little frightened. The next day, I learned, that I had a wonderful teacher and very nice classmates. I started very poorly. I think the sixth grade set me back, considerably.

As the months passed I gradually improved. The first quarter I received a pretty poor report card. My mother and father weren't very proud of me.

My teacher helped me very much. Her name was Miss O'Brien. The next report card was somewhat better. It still was not what I wanted. My teacher never gave up hope. She continued to help me. The next quarter, I really tried to do my job, and do it right. I received my report card last week and I was very happy to see, that there were all As and Bs. I took it home. My mother and father were very proud of me. They considered me their precious little lamb.

We live on a farm in District 10. We have many animals. We have chinchillas, one cow, a calf, dog, cat, and we are hoping to have chickens. I love the farm. It is where I always have wanted to live. While at home that night, I thought I'd catch up on all my work, so I went to bed about ten oclock that night. When I woke up and dawned my clothes, I thought I better hurry and milk the cow, so that I would not be late for school. I am trying my best to improve my work even more. As yet, I have a wonderful teacher and a very nice class, also a wonderful farm. Perhaps I just do not know when I am well off. I do appreciate my blessings. Philip Winans

***

Phil was a red-haired boy of fourteen in 1957, and his brother was two years older. They worked a couple of summers picking peaches near Marysville and saved up enough money to buy their own truck, which they drove to Montana to stay with their uncles at the ranch. Phil said he drove part of the way that summer, even though he didn't have a license. This was the ranch his mom grew up on, and the family still owned it, even though they also stayed in California most of the time.

I loved to hear Phil talk about his past. We'd be sitting in the living room in the evening, or sometimes on free afternoons we would lie on the bed and talk until we felt like taking naps. Phil told me how one time he figured out a way to do his ranch work and fish at the same time. First he drove the tractor once around the field he was mowing. Then, when he reached the side of the field bounded by Smoke Creek, he stopped the tractor. He scrambled down through the aspen, picked up his fishing pole, and fished until he caught something. It didn't take long, Phil said, because Smoke Creek was full of brook trout. After one fish was caught, he went up and did another circuit of the field with the mower. He spent a whole afternoon mowing and fishing all by himself and thinking all the time how smart he was to do both.

And oh, my, how I loved Phil's made up stories of a Montana wild horse bunch led by the clever stallion, RoughnTumble. Phil had written these stories in his mind before I met him, and as we lay snuggled in bed some cold winter afternoon, I would ask, "How is RoughnTumble doing?" Then Phil would tell me how the Indians tried to catch the stallion, but RoughnTumble led his herd, including RolyPoly and SteelDust and all the others (so many funny names like TospyTurvy, UpsyDaisy, TwirlAway) down the valley, and the Indians couldn't catch them, even when using rally ponies.

Phil listened to me as much or more than I listened to him; I remember telling him about my first horse, Stickshift (talk about funny names), the white-faced one-blue-eyed bay colt who bucked a friend off when she tried to train him, so I had to sell him and get Prieta, my old black mare I rode through my last days of adolescence, all over the hills and valleys of south Hemet. "Then after college, I was given a beautiful Arabian colt, a dark bay I named Don Diego," I told Phil. "Don Diego is the alter ego name of Zorro, you know, and Zorro was my childhood hero. Diego was a grandson of the very famous sire, Bask," I bragged. "I was so sorry to sell him, but I wasn't brave enough to be a horse trainer myself."

"There was a mare I rode," Phil told me in reply, "a quarter horse mare considered mine whenever I came out to the ranch; I'd known her since I was nine and just learning to ride. One summer Uncle Glen said I could have her colt, but I wasn't much for training horses, either. I had my uncle sell the colt, so I could have the money. Now I'm sorry I did that; the money was soon gone."

Then Phil told me a dramatic memory about once he was out rounding up cattle on his mare with his Uncle Bill, and Bill got too close to one of the bulls. The bull just plowed his horn into Bill's horse, and the horse fell over like it had been shot, and the bull ran on. Then Bill stood looking down on his favorite horse, who had blood flowing out of his shoulder. Phil said, "Bill told me to go get the shotgun, so I was riding back to the house, nearly sobbing about it. But when I came back, I saw that the horse had gotten up and was standing by Uncle Bill. Uncle Bill told me, 'I just can't do it; I can't shoot him.' So we called the vet, and the horse was fixed up. He wasn't much of a trail horse after that, but I was glad he didn't have to die."

"Uncle Bill committed suicide, didn't he?" I asked Phil.

"That was much later. He had problems in his marriage," Phil answered. I never knew too much about Bill, but wished I did. Did he have similar problems to Phil's, I wondered.

Phil told me a nice memory about a time when he rode his horse up into the forest above the ranch. He spotted a buck with a large rack standing nearby and gazing at him. Phil pulled up his mare, and they stood facing the deer about ten yards away. The deer took a few steps toward them, so Phil nudged his horse forward. The two animals gingerly approached one another, while Phil held his breath.

"The deer and my horse and I regarded each other a long time, and when I went past toward home again, I looked back and saw that the deer was following me. He followed my horse and me a long way. But the buck stayed at the top of the hill, finally," Phil finished. "I kept turning around in the saddle; I could see the deer standing just at the edge of the trees, watching me as I rode back to the ranch."

"That's beautiful, Philly," I said, sitting up against his side on the couch, snuggling. It was the perfect ending for a story I soon wrote using these memories of Montana, which was published at the beginning of the university magazine, with many other writers' good stories and poems following.

Phil's memories, why did I love them so? And how many were there that I never heard? Somehow it was hard for me to get over the fact that any one human being, such as Phil, had a lifetime wrapped up inside him from one memory to the next, so large in quantity that I could never know him completely.

***

I don't know for sure, but I believe Phil's mental illness (ultimately diagnosed as schizoaffective disorder) began in his late teens. He told me he went right out of high school into the Air Force, from the influence of a friend of his dad's who had been in the services. My guess is that parents and other loved ones around Phil were vaguely aware of his trouble and thought that the Air Force would help him. Though he traveled to Greenland, learned to be a boiler operator, had friends, and was honorably discharged, he left early because of his illness coming to the forefront.

Of his twenties and early thirties I know only a little - his first marriage, his girlfriends, his travels around the country, his tries at careers and higher learning, his spells of illness, his own thoughts of suicide (he told me once he had gone to a gun shop and ordered a rifle, but then never went to pick it up). He also joined the G. I. Gurdjieff group in San Francisco, which was a historic way of enlightenment, or a cult, depending on how you looked at it. One of the books he wanted me to read at the beginning of our courtship was *Meetings With Remarkable Men*, by Gurdjieff, which I found a fascinating book. Later he discounted the Gurdijeff experience, as it reminded him, I think, of his ill times.

Of the papers I have found in Phil's boxes in the garage, some are comprehensible and some are not. But I think it is clear his mind was working on questions of the meaning of life, education, and the odd paradox of being one thing and the opposite at the same time (as I understand it). I can see the intelligence and even part of the meaning in his ideas, but I think some quirk of the deep down psychosis interferes with his ability to communicate completely.

His idea of the Interpreter went through several stages. Here is just one explanation.

THE INTERPRETER

The interpreter is a machine and an idea that took me many years to invent. As a play it is done by the actors and the resisters. The actors are making a story that is real. The resistors are the audience that tries to resist this true story for an untrue story. Some plays go entirely to the actors and some go entirely to the audiences. To the extent that they compare, they are either true or imaginary. Knowing the way the truth is made real or false is in their conscience.

There needs to be at least two plays to compare, but there could be many more. The way the plays are compared is done by using one's reason in the form of exactitudes. The memory of these exactitudes and how they will vary from individual to individual becomes the history of one's reason - one's individuality. Of course different players will have different reasons based on many different ideas, including their references - that is, what they bring to the play from the past.

When not a play, the Interpreter could be a game acted out to form the different behaviors. You resist in this way so you can overcome one's opponent - actual or computer opponent. I feel that television and theaters of the future will go this way. When you have two plays going at one time your attention gets divided, so thinking can go on...

***

When Phil saw the popularity of computer games in the nineties, he sought a way to turn the Interpreter into a series of space games with science fiction background stories to make them interesting. He spent an inspired and frenzied year typing story after story, page-long adventures of the people called the Omrah and their men machines, which were ancestors converted into very active robots that sometimes fought and sometimes didn't believe in fighting. Ultimately, after trying to sell these stories to a game maker and being ignored, Phil and I decided I would take his stories and make them into a sci-fi novel, of which I completed 12 chapters before I wrote myself into a hole, which I haven't tried to get out of yet.

Introduction TO THE OMRAH PEOPLE

Once there was a people called the Omrah. The people of the Omrah regarded their dead very differently than most people do. Because of their vast technology and their understanding of gravity they were able to preserve their dead in an uncommon way. The dead were preserved as machines, or robots, called Minmah. Each of the Minmah was different in reason and conscience and was able to retain their individuality. They resembled human figures, but were made of a special metal that helped them to be much stronger and more agile than the living people.

The men machines had been made over a long period of time, thirteen hundred years, and so quite naturally they increased the population of each planet by thousands. They were kept in great caves called tombs where they could be activated from time to time to be used in learning plays. They also helped the Omrah by doing jobs in the world, such as journeying through space.

The Omrah mingled with their Minmah very freely, since the education of the Omrah children and youth was left up to these machines. Everything learned had to be acted out with other people on the great stages inside the tombs. The Omrah dead were stored here in the tombs, also, and their gravity machines were stored in them as well.

The Omrah used to believe in offensive or defensive actions against others, but the recent generations did not believe even in self defense. Their consciences were highly evolved by these learning plays of theirs. So according to the Minmah generations, some were very protective of the Omrah and would defend them, and yet other generations who were more developed, didn't believe in self defense. (This will lead to exciting adventures in the depths of space as the Omrah and Minmah explore beyond their own world.)

Omrah - The Mind of Odoot

Emote is investigating a geometrical being that has appeared near the Omrah planet of Zempo. At first Emote is frightened, but then decides to be brave and risk everything to know this geometrical being of many shining lights. There is an opening, so Emote enters and is shocked by changing shapes of similar first, then different objects. She finds this contradiction familiar and exciting. She senses that she might be lost and found in the same moment.

She hears a voice say:

This is the mind of Odoot - the beginning and the end of knowledge. The beginning ends, but the end never does. That which is the same ends and that which is different never does. That which ends is the beginning of not the end but only the beginning of forever, forever to know and grow understanding. My universe is always becoming the end but never approaches it, for that would be the beginning.

I am one very different or I am one and the same number of differences. In me you can know forever on occasion. Now you are one, there is hope in one for you, though you can remember afterward and never know how much. Or if you are not one you can never comprehend no matter how much you remember. You will be here for a little while and yes, you can remember.

To know one is simple. To know difference is wise. Now you will be here forever or for a short while - it is up to your faith and doubt. Without conscience you are lost. But who would not be lost? Which is the less of two evils, to know evil as comprehensible or incomprehensible? Yet many can be comprehended to be one and the same and one different a number of times. You see forever is all around us, yet forever could not happen.

***

Sometimes I'd look curiously at Phil as we sat in our living room, and I'd ask him, "What are you thinking?" I don't know if it was the truth, but his reply was often, "I'm thinking about the Bible." We didn't discuss religion that much. He knew I didn't like it, and I knew he had his own way, which I respected. When Phil was unwell, his religion was mean and convoluted, but when he was well, it became kind and true. Sometimes he told me it didn't matter that I didn't believe, that he would take care of me in that regard, to which I would smile and say thank you.

When Phil felt his worst psychologically, which happened in my presence maybe four or five times in 24 years, (usually from not taking his medicines, but other times for some unknown-to-me reason) one of his symptoms was to become ultra religious. I found some writings which Phil might have written when he was especially troubled.

To Have Not the World

To have not the world as anybody's reward
To reap its temptation in some unearned way
To decide to win
To decide to lose

"Oh, My Redwood Heart!"

One cannot escape by being the other
And there is not one innocent enough to get away.

The simple see so they can understand
The wise understand so they can see
When the wise fail to understand, they cannot see
When the simple fail to see, they have faith
In what happened that they don't know;
They may be filled with what they don't know -
That is their knowledge - Faith.

A Fragment --
From a school from a study from a world of excitement from a voice that never asked for help to a place to see all sorts of things to the end of the end - to gladly exchange my whole size and shape for any as different as the same - from large to very small I think it is -- From now as from no beginning - for there is no where to begin.

"You are educable," said a voice that quickly fled away.

I was identified and felt my heart slipping away after the voice, and I became just one inch tall.

"To learn is to know questions, and if something happens you understand what you did not know." The voice spoke again.

"Nothing happens to me any more," I replied, in a wee voice.

"If you are tired of being here I can take you where there is nothing like anything. To be lost is to know the way."

And so as I was never myself anymore, I followed away, approaching what seemed to be one and the same place, for that was the only way we could go.

***

When we first began telling each other about ourselves,

47

Debbie Bumstead

Phil told me his Native American name would be "Broken Wing." I asked what it meant to him, and he explained, "Because I want to fly, but I can't - I have a broken wing." I believe this was Phil's understanding of himself deep inside.

He had unique ways of describing his state, and sometimes I remembered the quotes and noted them down in my journal.

*I'm unplugged; I don't have current anymore.

*I'm like a sandwich with nothing in between - cause and effect with nothing of myself in between.

*What's really important is what you'd live for again.

*I love him more than telling would do. (This in grieving for his younger brother who died of cancer at 43)

*I feel like an actor who hasn't got any lines.

*Everything I am is like a sheet flying outside the window.

I also liked some of the things he said to me.

*You're so hurt, you are even hurt when you are what you think you want to be.

*You're so young and tender; I'm so old and settled.

*Think of yourself as loved.

*You're so little and involved.

Here are some fragments Phil spoke while musing on the seasons:

*In Autumn the land is finished
And the window looks --

*In winter Nature is disturbed by expectation.

*In winter trees outnumber the leaves.

Phil and I used other sayings, too, as jokes or statements. One we said often, when circumstances warranted, was a sentence that a first grade boy had me write under a photo of a large stag in the forest:

*The hunter is a killer.

Some others:

* Soooo, you're the one they call the Hep Cat! - Phil's dad said this when we visited him as he lay dying, and we used it often in greeting each other afterwards.

*I'm leaving it all up to youooooo! - I'd sing this line sometimes to make Phil laugh.

*I like a man with a slow hand… - Another line from a song that described Phil to me, and made him smile.

*Here we are - off to the Ugly Bug Ball! - As I mentioned before, when we got dressed up, we'd say this line from a Burl Ives song.

*It isn't easy being green.. Sometimes we would quote Kermit the Frog when we felt we didn't live up to what we wanted of ourselves.

*Don't hurt me now… - another song line

*Philly - I loved to call Phil Philly in tender moments.

And Phil loved it when I told him that while he was taking a nap one day, he sang out in his sleep:

*Oh, my Redwood Heart!

Debbie Bumstead

Part Two

Debbie Bumstead

❧Alice Street Thank Account ❧
1987 - Medford, Oregon

August 9, 1987 Sunday - I'm thankful for the pleasant air that breathes over me as I sit on the lounge here on our lawn. The green of the hedge, the rose bushes, the grass, the black oak which I'm facing, all of this green I like, and also, the sun as it sets and the gold light it puts on the house walls in patterns.

I'm thankful for the house itself, the living room and its four big windows, my study which I've just arranged with a brick and board bookcase, our bedroom with its new king-size bed, the laundry room with the washer and dryer my mother gave us, the bathroom with its hot water, and the kitchen.

I'm thankful for my marriage, companionship, and friendship with Phil, and in particular for our long bike ride in the cool of the morning down the Sunday quiet streets to the park downtown. We rested on the bench under the huge green trees, planted, we guessed, at the town's beginning, and watched the foraging blackbirds. Phil was kind to go to the store with me, and later he sat with his hand on my knee as we watched television.

Today I read in the mystery, *The Woman in White* by Wilkie Collins.

I have a lot of free time during these days before my school librarian classes start at the college in Ashland, but I'm thankful to have those classes ahead of me. They give me an aim, a purpose, to go forward.

August 10, 1987 Monday - I am alive, l am able to feel both happiness and sadness, I am able to see the tree-covered hills, the farm land, the small houses that I like to look at on our drives to Ashland - as we drove there today. I am able to hear, to feel, to smell; I am able to be myself.

August 11, 1987 Tuesday - I'm thankful for the morning and the way in which I wake up. I don't have to hurry. I can stay dozing beside Phil. I can go have my bowl of cereal on the couch - that is what I did today - and read while I eat.

This morning I wrote to my mother and also to the literary agency trying to sell my book. My mother is a nice friend and someone I still rely on to confide in things. She is coming to visit in a week and a half.

As for the literary agency, they have taken on my book; that's something. One of the greatest things to me is my accomplishment of writing my novel.

I like the Medford library with its books up and down the rows and around the walls that Phil and I visited today.

The weather is sunny but not too hot. The lazy days are restful and help me ready myself for busier times. It's hard to know what I do all day, but I am thankful for that leisurely nothing-much-ness. When the evening comes, as it has now, I see the blue twilight beyond the curtains and hear the sound of the neighbor calling her dog, Pierre. I think of Phil in the other room who keeps me from being lonely.

August 12, 1987 Wednesday - Let me list those things for which I am thankful today.

1. The revelation I had in the middle of the night. Waking up suddenly, I had the alert recognition that I was on the right track. l should work toward the school librarian certificate. I

shouldn't worry at the moment about writing for publication; I should let my novel work on that for me.

2. The drive Phil and I took down to Ashland and out Highway 64 into the country. We saw hilly grassy forested country with clean plain homes and shiny horses in pastures and a creek, full of trout, Phil said, and Emigrant Lake. We said we'd like to live there, and that thought led to:

3. The daydream I had on the way home about having twin red-headed boys named Glenn and Gregory and a country home outside Ashland. I dreamed a girlfriend came to visit us and as I drove her in from the airport, the two boys jumped and waved in the front yard as we came home. Phil took care of the children while my friend and I took a horseback ride down to the creek.

4. The fun I had chasing and being chased by Monty the cat in the house and how our fun made Phil smile.

5. The scrapbook I made from some of the photos I've cut out of magazines and collected in my file cabinet.

6. Once again the weather.

7. Once again my mystery.

8. The pink roses blooming in the rose hedge around our yard. Every time I go outside, it strikes me that our roses are wonderful to see.

9. Dear friend, husband, Phil, and our efforts to fill the days. Sometimes we are successful, sometimes not, but either way I'm thankful we have each other and the ability to try.

August 13, 1987 Thursday - There are wonderful trees to see in this town of Medford, in the nice neighborhood east of downtown that Phil and I drove around today. We have daydreams of me being a school librarian and him a counselor and us having a nice house like the ones we saw.

I love Phil, my friends and relatives, and the world when it is beautiful.

Debbie Bumstead

August 15, 1987 Saturday - Though I should not be too thankful for a sensational murder mystery book like *Where Are the Children?*, I am thankful for the way a book like that helps pass time.

My mother called me today and told me the news that she will be up next Saturday.

Phil was in good spirits today. We bought him jeans at K-mart.

The water turns in circles from the sprinkler over the lawn. Holly plays with a squeaky toy on the grass. And indoors, the funny cat, Pie, sits on the couch between Phil and me as if she wanted to be close, but as soon as we pet her, she tries to bite us, making us laugh.

August 20, 1987 - Phil and I are able to treat each other gently, cheerfully, patiently, and lovingly through these long do-nothing days.

September 11, 1987 - Over the past weeks many things have happened to be thankful for. My mother visited us. She took the bus through the forests to Medford. On Saturday my mother and I went to the Church of Christ, and afterwards Phil took us to the Wild Plum for lunch. Monday was wonderful. Mama had the idea for a picnic at Emigrant Lake, so we fixed sandwiches, fruit, drinks, homemade ice cream, and cookies, packed them up into the ice chest, took a blanket and pillows, the lawn lounge, and our books and magazines to a table on the green hill under the oaks and overlooking the lake.

I loved hearing the squeals of the children at the water slide behind us. I loved the shore walk Phil and I took over the hill to see more of the lake. I loved lying in the dappled shade on the blanket reading and dozing, being content, and knowing Phil and my mother were content, too.

We shopped in Jacksonville and at the Mall on Tuesday, and Mama found some things to buy for herself and others.

Phil started a conversation with Mama, and we heard interesting stories of: her Uncle Comer and Uncle Frank being hobos on trains, and getting jobs at a box factory in Portola; then their parents (my great-grandparents) moving to join them and then Grandmother, Grandpa, and Mama (high school age) moving from Alabama to join, too; Grandpa getting a job with the Southern Pacific Railroad in Reno, and then Grandmother becoming the ticket lady at the SP Station; Mama going to college at Pepperdine where she met my Daddy; and then about the Wagon Wheel Motel being built in Reno. That's where Phil and I came to meet forty years later!

Mama left for home on the bus on Wednesday.

I've read two good books: *Growing Up* by Russel Baker and *A Life of Her Own* by Mare Brandel.

I'm thankful for Phil's friendship and love, and I'm thankful for all the things there are to do in life.

September 23, 1987 - Wednesday - I want to go back into the past. My name is Mary Deborah Alice Bumstead Winans. I am five feet six inches tall, with light brown hair cut short and dark blue eyes. I wear glasses and I'm not pretty. I don't want to complain, but it is true; I was never pretty or beautiful. My life up to now could be summarized in this way: I had a happy childhood interspersed with periods of fear and loneliness and a miserable adolescence interspersed with moments of happiness. My adult life I look on as a series of steps forward, college one step, working around my hometown one step, moving to Reno and going back to college another step, getting married another, and moving here to Oregon with plans for getting a librarian's certificate one more step. Steps I foresee for the future are: working in a school library, one step, buying our own home, another step, accomplishing my goals as a writer and being published, one giant step.

September 26, 1987 - I finished reading *The Borrowers Afield* by Mary Norton, and started *The Borrowers Aloft*.

I sat on the couch with the heating pad around my middle all morning with cramps. Later sat out on the lounge on the lawn with Holly. Beautiful beautiful fall day.

Phil practiced on the piano he'd rented last week, watered the lawn, sat and thought, went to the market for milk, candy, and aspirin.

I watched *Greyfriar's Bobby*, News, *Rockford Files* with Phil, and then Phil watched a movie, *Return to Dodge*, while I read in the bedroom.

September 27, 1987 - I went with Phil to the Country Store and the bank. We washed the car. I played with Holly, napped with Phil, looked at photos in one of our albums, and daydreamed. Weather: a little haze but beautiful.

September 28, 1987 - Monday - I drove to Ashland to attend the college classes I'd been waiting months to begin. But I decided to drop the idea of going to school. I suffered with my decision the rest of the day. I worked on a resume for a job search.

Phil mowed the lawn, spent the day supporting me with my change of heart. We watched news, *Wheel of Fortune*, *Frank's Place*, and a movie *Star Trek III*.

Weather beautiful, leaves are going golden.

Epilogue of 1987 - So how could I fault Phil for trying to go somewhere to try something new and then failing, when I did the same? I remember that Monday in September 1987 vividly. I drove to Ashland from Medford in the morning, full of eagerness to pursue my goal of being a school librarian. On the highway I saw a cat that had been hit by a car. It staggered in the middle of the road, saliva dripping from its mouth. The sight made me feel awful. Then I reached the college, but I couldn't find a parking place. I parked high up a hill and had to hike down a long way, so that I ached badly by the time I got to my first class. Then, I got a blow from the professor: oral reports were part of the syllabus. I dreaded oral reports and could foresee a whole year of them, twelve classes of them, coming up. I ached so much I couldn't withstand my loss of willpower, and I came home broken. I regret that bad day. I wish I could have gone on; how I wish I could have. But Phil understood.

Debbie Bumstead

⚡Gridley Days ⚡
1988-89 Memories

In the spring of 1988 Phil and I took a scouting trip to Gridley, California, population about 4000. It was a pretty day, cool and sunny, and we took a room in one of the two motels we saw outside town. Then we drove to the old downtown, which had just been improved with maple trees and parking areas. Phil kept saying he wished the building his parents had seen for a furniture store was on the main highway. But the empty old red brick Penney's was on a corner right downtown beside a clothing store, across from a gift shop, there in the quiet part of Gridley, away from the fast highway that ran from Chico down to Marysville, the freeways and Sacramento.

It was exciting, though, to be with Phil walking along the street, gauging the building from this point and that, imagining what it'd be like to have a store of our own. When we got back to talk to Phil's parents, Phil said he wasn't sure it would go. "It isn't on the main highway, and there's a bigger furniture store south of town that is on the highway," Phil said. But Dad said that didn't matter; he wanted to start another furniture store and that was the place.

**

A month later Phil was in Gridley helping with the cleaning up of the building, and I was in Reno, ready to join Phil and his parents, to drive up over the Donner Pass down

60

into California. It was April, clear in Reno, and I didn't worry about the weather, but as I drove our orange Fiesta up to Truckee, it began to snow. I pulled over on the highway, wondering if I should go on. But if I didn't, how would I turn around? So I went on.

The snow fell heavier and heavier, sticking to the pavement, making the world white on either side, piling into drifts, silently challenging me. I was afraid. Other drivers weren't so shy as I; they passed me, spurting up snow. Then I got l behind a truck that was going slowly, and I stayed behind him right over the mountain. It was strange to be driving, my muscles all tense, my heart beating hard, and out in the beautiful forest the snow falling quietly.

I came down from the mountains into the rainy valley. When I reached Gridley, I pulled in front of the Penney's and saw Phil helping to carry old things belonging to the landlady out of the building. I hugged him, and then began to cry; I was so relieved to be done with my fearful drive. Phil was a little embarrassed, since there were people all around, but I was comforted by his presence, just to see his bigness and strength, and the way he carved out the air around him with his being. He gave me the key to his room, so I went there to rest and fell asleep for awhile.

**

We rented a house on Spruce Street. It had used to be the place the ambulance had its headquarters, so there was a large parking area, and indoors the kitchen and back room were clean with new linoleum. We had a small living room and two small bedrooms with one bathroom. The yard was just grass with a huge pine tree on one side and in back lots of vines and bushes. It was a public sort of house, right on a bare corner on a busy street, and yet we liked it. The school bus stop was nearly in our yard, so that neighborhood children gathered there every morning.

Phil's Mom and Dad gave us the furniture that they had in

storage: a comfortable sofa and loveseat and a queen bed for the extra room. As time went on, we also acquired a dinette, coffee table and lamp tables, a bedroom suite, and three fine dark wood bookcases to house my vintage book collection. Phil's parents soon found a house to rent, too, down the street from us, a three bedroom tract-style place, and they got new furniture for it. Why not? We owned a furniture store!

**

The store had two big areas, one which we used for sofas, recliners, and dining tables, the other which was the Sleep Shop with beds and bedroom furniture. A counter was built at the far end of the store facing the two doors, and we four sat there waiting for customers. There were raised platforms in the front windows which were decorated like pretend rooms, the largest one in the middle with an expensive sofa and lamp tables. In a way it was fun to check out the furniture, sitting in the chairs and sofas throughout the store, testing them, though at first Phil's dad disapproved. But as the store slowly failed, he didn't care about much, even smoked in the store and let his ashes fall on the floor.

On the day of our Grand Opening, a radio station brought its remote, along with a huge blow-up cowboy that they couldn't get to stand up, so he sat on the sidewalk by our door. Free hotdogs were handed out, and when people came in they were given a free gift, a silver-plated platter or a clock. I remember the two homeless-looking men in smelly old raggedy clothes that came in wanting their free gift, and we sent them on their way, each holding a shining silver platter.

The business went along OK, though it was nerve-wracking to sit in the store all day some days with no one coming in. I liked taking the money we'd made to the bank each day, and I liked filling in the books and filing the sales receipts. I liked walking up the block with Phil for our break to The Bronze Cue. The Cue had a small counter in front of the greasy grill, and we sat there and ate doughnuts. Phil lit up a cigarette, and the cook told him he didn't look like the kind of guy who smoked.

He didn't, and for a year he had been off cigarettes, but I remember the day Phil began to smoke again. I guess after constant exposure to his dad's cigarettes at the store, he one day lit up. I was so upset about it, I left in tears. I hiked around the back corner and up Spruce toward home. As I passed the abandoned building beside the alley, I nearly ran into the town's new Reverend. He said sorry in his own wimpy way, and I went on, crying quietly, wondering what he thought of me.

It sounds like I was a real crybaby, and maybe so I was; crying was my reaction to every physical or mental hurt I felt. I took an antidepressant that was supposed to help me with the fibromyalgia and a pill to help with cramps. Phil still took several different meds, which the VA sent to him in the mail. Every few months we had to make a trip to Reno to visit his doctors. For almost a year Phil kept it together; he was as healthy as I'd ever known him. Whether it was helping his parents that made him well, or the idea of having his own furniture store one day, or the physical work of delivering, or a combination, Phil was the man he and I wanted him to be, and it was good.

The Reverend and his wife were new to one of the churches in town. They came in to buy some chairs, and I went with Phil to deliver them. I liked going on deliveries with Phil, which we did often, not being able to hire a boy fulltime. And I loved the times that Mom and Dad left us in charge of the store, on Saturdays and on days they went to visit relatives. Then it seemed like the store was really our own. I could relax, not have to worry what Dad wanted of me, not have to worry about keeping up a conversation with Mom. One Saturday Phil and I sold a recliner to Laura, a friendly old woman who had been walking by our store day after day. Phil and I were so excited to have sold a chair all by ourselves!

**

I soon begged Phil to let me work part-time. Now my stomach was bothering me terribly and my menstrual cramps affected me half the month, it seemed. Phil and his parents agreed I wasn't needed all day, so by about Christmas I was only going in to work two hours at lunchtime. Mom and Dad would go off to eat, and I'd catch up on the paperwork, then sit around with Phil. I was much happier. Afterwards I'd go home, write, shop, keep house, and wait for Phil to come home from work. I was a wife!

As we had always done wherever we lived, we drove around a lot on our time off from work. We drove around Gridley looking at homes, also to nearby Biggs, which was even smaller than Gridley. We went out to Phil's cousin's cabin near the river, over to his aunt's property in Lincoln, over to Oroville to look at another store building, and then to Chico for dinner or to the library there. I'll never forget the beautiful sight of the walnut grove we drove through east of Gridley in the middle of Autumn. We drove for two or three miles with just the trees on either side of us, all golden-leaved, and on the earth more gold from the leaves that had fallen already.

One evening during a Presidential Gala on TV, Phil and I were pulled into the magic of *The Music of the Night*. Michael Crawford's strange haunting voice flowed over us as we both stood in the middle of the living room, stopped in our tracks from doing some odd job. The very next day, a day off, we drove into Chico to find the *Phantom of the Opera* album to play on our stereo. So many lines from the *Phantom* seemed to fit my love for Phil, about the times he seemed to hide, a pitiful creature of darkness, and how I so wanted to show him he was not alone. At the same time, here in Gridley especially, he was also like Christine's young prince, strong, protective, full of physical warmth.

Phil working, me helping, our own business, our house, a

small town, interesting characters, visiting relatives, drives with just the two of us together, this made our time in Gridley the best time of our marriage to me, despite my health. But Phil's nerves finally began to hurt him. After a year or so, he couldn't bear to see the business slowly failing. We abandoned it to his parents who had to see it out through the two year lease. We went back to Reno. I remember the green trees around our house in Reno, how they blew in the summer breezes, the air lighter, cooler, drier than the hot humid summer of Gridley, and how Phil felt a great sense of relief and pleasure at being done with furniture.

❧The Five Year Diaries ❧
1990-1999

The two five-year diaries I kept in the 90s are disappointing. Each entry is small to fit in, so I just wrote what we did each day -- and what did we do? Cycles of the same things, never going forward, always caught in a pattern that never changed. We lived in the house on the hill above the Wagon Wheel again, the very house that used to be the duplex where Phil and I met. Now we had the whole house, two bedrooms, two bathrooms, a living room and a kitchen and laundry. I worked for the University again, part-time. Phil often had guard jobs, but not for long. I felt like I was writing some good books, but they weren't good enough to get published. Phil felt like he had good ideas of inventions and businesses, but nothing came of them, either.

Interspersed in the mundane entries are periods of misery, for both Phil and me. Phil's illness, I think, caused a very deep suffering inside him that drove him to attempt escape. The easiest escape seemed to be to move physically, to take off. I had gone with him a few times, but now I decided I had to stay in Reno and just be terribly lonely while he was away. Later in our marriage, after many more brief vacations Phil took in his search for success, I would question myself: was I like a battered woman, always taking back my man? Phil was gentleness personified. He rarely showed his temper - actually

I was more temperamental than he, despite my shyness. But I did feel battered by his discontent that came in waves: first an idea occurred to him; then he began to talk of moving to here or there; then he'd take his SSD money and have me drive him to the bus station, and off he'd go. Of course, he soon ran out of money, and came back, but I still felt maddened when, after a pleasant period where he was content at home, he'd have another idea and make another escape!

Those short trips he made on his own were not the worst. When he became extremely depressed, to the point of imagining people didn't like him or thinking he would be better off dead, then he would need his mother. He'd travel up to Oregon and stay, both before and after his dad died, for two or three months. It sounds funny, that a big tall grown up man, so strong in body and so wise in mind, would become so scared a child that he had to go back to the safest person he knew. I wasn't that person. It was his mom, Doris. I'd feel lonely, maybe a little angry and jealous, but I understood. I guessed it was so in every human, that deep down place of fear, but in those with some illnesses, the deep comes tumbling up so easily to the top. I knew it in myself.

When Doris moved back to Fallon, about an hour from Reno, to be near her daughter, things improved. We'd drive out to see her, or she would come to stay with us a few days. She was the one person I could talk to about Phil. One day when just we two were driving in town, she exclaimed, "Why does he have to go through such torture?" She meant the torture Phil suffered when he thought he was on the right track, that his idea was the greatest, and would be successful and make him millions, that was the torture he didn't recognize himself until all went bust. And the torture of never learning from these lessons! Maybe all of us are hopeful and try again when we fail, but in Phil's case, he went too high in his mind and fell too far in his failure, and then repeated the process, sometimes with the very same idea. How could a genius man be so clueless? I'd think, though critical thoughts like that always made me question and recognize my own endless trials and errors of life.

*Dear Friend *
1990 - Selected Journal Entries

1990 - January
Dear Friend,
Who are you? An imaginary friend who lives far far away, on another planet; yes, up in the quietness of space, somewhere in that endless universe, I see you waiting to know me. From your perspective I imagine the earth to be an exotic place fascinating to learn about, and me, your special interest, your pen-pal, your hobby, your class project, your potential for great knowledge of a single common human being, even more so.

I had a thought several weeks ago that comes back to me sometimes as I go out to town and see or speak to people. The thought was this: the world teems with people, individuals, billions, is it, yet despite this knowledge we have of there being so many people on earth that we aren't as important as we'd like, we still look at each other, relatives, friends, co-workers, acquaintances, each of us looks at the other with interest, whether we are friendly or mean, and we recognize and accept the individual importance of each other. That seems amazing to me, considering the quantity of people in the world, some famous, some starving to death, some leading unhappy lives, some being criminals, all speaking different languages, hundreds, thousands, millions, billions. As soon as one in a billion meets another in a billion there are questions asked, stories shared, experiences compared, as if those two in a billion were important! I like that. It saves me and all the other billions from feeling too much like meaningless bits of fluff in the universe.

**

Here is a life for you: books on shelves, dolls in cupboards, china animals arranged in parties, files full of papers, a shelf of personal writings, a carpet that spreads throughout a house, a bathroom with a bathtub full of bubbles, golden oak living room tables and brass lamps and soft couches with a husband sitting surrounded by love, a TV full of movies, a stereo singing the Phantom, a dinette under an Indian picture of coyotes leaping in the sky, a kitchen with chicken, spaghetti, muffins, cereal, and milk, milk, milk, a bedroom full of bed, a dresser full of pullovers, a shower hot and long, a toothbrush for a strong pair of choppers, a comb for short brown hair, a mirror that looks back at a plain face and deep eyes, deep, deep eyes that even the owner can't see the end of, a back room full of old hobbies, tools, a washer, a dryer; this is a life with many doors to the outside, wooden and glass, doors nailed shut and doors with bad locks, and outdoors full of trees and dead grass and gravel driveways and junk in piles and motel rooms filled with men, an outdoors with roads that lead away and come back, a life of meeting people, glancing away, smiling helplessly, working efficiently in the background, and wishing, wishing, wishing. That's a life for you.

**

Phil and I drove south on MacCarren around to the area of homes on the hills above the city. In one area we have seen houses like mansions with windows at all corners and chimneys as wide as walls, and garages, three in a row for one place. But today we looked at more established homes, smaller, lower to the ground, surrounded by evergreen, and seemingly more attainable. "I want to get you a house like this and have it all paid for," Phil said. "Then you'll have a home after I go." Die, he meant. But I am not afraid. The sun warms me, makes me easy, makes me feel like not striving, like relaxing, like letting myself be, and being contented.

Your Friend, Debbie

****

February
Dear Friend,

It snowed on my birthday, a monster storm of 19 inches in Reno alone, six or eight feet in the mountains. The power went off in the evening; Phil and I lighted candles and huddled in blankets, discovering the true nature of our drafty house - how mean it is in winter without its heater going. Now we are snowbound, unable to get the car out of the driveway. We walked along the icy street to 7/11 for milk and a paper for Grandpa and a cake to bake for my birthday. Trudging through the knee-deep snow back and forth to the motel has given me an arthritic pain in the hip with fire up and down my left leg. I'm sorry for myself and cry. I am 36 years old with the achy bones of a seventy year old, doesn't seem fair. But, I have a husband to love, a job to enjoy, a home to keep me warm - when the power is on - and a dear friend to write to, you.

**

Reno winters go on and on. Phil and I get cupcakes and chocolate at the 7/11, drive across to San Rafael Park, park above the ranch house, and sit in the car and look out over the rolling hills and the ravine where a stream wanders through. The elms lining the drive are bare, tall, a distinct impression on my mind. Trees are so often noticeable and yet so quiet and apart from human busy-ness. And the wild geese wheel in flocks across the cold sky, coming in for a landing with their wide webbed feet sticking comically forward.

**

Sometimes I feel as if life ought to click, mysteries ought to be cleared up; we should know the answers to make ourselves better, wiser. I felt this at age eleven in a summer school science class. We were shown a poster of the insides of a human and had to learn the names of all the bones in the body. I thought I was learning the answers to life itself. I had the same thought in my ninth grade Life Science class. I thought if only I could learn enough, some day everything I knew would click into place and I'd understand. Even now I feel as if I could get to the bottom of the mystery if only I learned enough about - what? - plants, animals, the earth, the stars. If I could put together all the amazing details, I might know the answer. I wonder if you can know from your quiet place in space how beautiful the world is? On second thought, maybe you know, from your perspective, even better than we do.

Your Friend, Debbie

****

March
Dear Friend,

This morning I stood at the glass door and watched as flocks of blackbirds rose across the sky from the south and passed over our hill in a rush. They made me feel glad, even happy. On my walk down to the motel, I saw an owl flap silently toward the canyon north of us.

There's a buoyant feeling in the air during the change of the season. The air itself reminds me of past times, here in this place or there in that one; every place I have lived, I guess, I have felt the same feelings, and so I am reminded of them all when I again feel the buoyant air of the changing earth. One day when I lived alone in the country corner house before Phil came back from Utah to court me, I walked into the bathroom there in that house and looked out the window across the weedy field in back, and I had a strange feeling. As if my life, my real life, were somewhere secret, in some wild beautiful place, not here in the human world I pretend I live in. It was a very true feeling, as if my real life goes on somewhere else in a real world I'm only able to glimpse at odd moments. Most of the time I'm caught up here in a business of getting by. It's an interesting business, but not real, and not really important, I think.

**

Have I introduced you to our animal family? Start with Holly, the Australian Cattle Dog, since she's the oldest. She is three-quarter sister to Rex, who died in 1986. Rex, the Dog Hero, I'd rather tell you about Rex, how he saved my life one day in the Hemet hills by going first around a rock and getting the rattlesnake bite instead of me - and survived it - and how he won ribbons and trophies in the obedience shows, how he protected me and acted as the man around the house when I was single, and finally how he helped me meet Phil, Rex's double in human form with the same red hair and dark cherrywood eyes, as we played on the lawn in front of our duplex. As for Holly, she is smart and sassy, fox-faced, and ever-ready.

Phil got Bridget last fall as a tiny puppy. He wanted a "Buddy" like the Boston Terrier that used to come visit him when he was working in Fallon at tearing down a house. This tough little Buddy dog would pick up a huge stick and carry it proudly. So Phil and I went to look at two puppies, both females. Phil wanted a boy pup, but he chose Bridget as his buddy anyway. She's funny and tough, but sweet, and she's cute like a bug or a gargoyle.

We have two cats, Monty, who is ten or eleven years old, and came from Hemet - he is big, half Siamese, my pal, a good friend, sociable, a kick-back kind of fellow with a sense of humor. His striped gray coat is thick and rich in the winter and smells cold and wild when he comes in from the night. I hug him with my cheek against his body. He purrs. But you know, he is more than just having a cat that purrs. He's been around so long, and developed from such a scrawny, but individual cat with personality plus, that he is almost like a person inside an animal body. He looks at me intelligently.

Then there's Pie, an odd little black and orange tortoiseshell, a barn cat, given to me by a college classmate here about six years ago. Pie's tiny like a perpetual kitten and though she hates to be petted, she's always around, lying on my lap, or begging in the kitchen, or nosing under the covers when I take a nap.

Your Friend, Debbie

****

April
Dear Friend,

April 1, 1990 - I am a fool, so this is my day.

On April I, 1980, just a month before moving to Reno and meeting Phil, I was driving the orange Fiesta through the hills between Beaumont and Hemet in California. Grandbee and Grandpa and Daddy were in the car with me, and we belonged to a long line of cars all cleaned and with headlights on, a funeral procession. We drove to the Hemet Cemetery to see my cousin Linda's coffin lowered into the ground, her "green pastures." She had become depressed (Linda also suffered childhood sex abuse from our Uncle Hersey) and had killed herself, leaving Bob and the three children, my second cousins I loved so much, Scott, Steve, and Christy.

Though I used to think of suicide up to that point as a possible solution, myself, after Linda's I saw that it was a big mistake. I'm grateful to her, though I wish she hadn't gone, because since then I haven't been so troubled with wondering whether I should die rather than suffer and struggle with life. I continue to suffer and struggle, but I'm not so grim about it.

Your Friend, Debbie

****

May
Dear Friend,

When Phil comes in from work in the morning and goes to bed, sometimes I lie down to keep him company for awhile. I look across the room at the National Geographic map on the wall, a map of the solar system with all the planets, except for Pluto, shown true to life by the Voyager photos, and arranged in a curve with the size of each planet in comparison to the others. Earth is small but beautiful.

I like to look at that map. It makes me feel better, as if the greatness of the universe will endure, while the pettiness of my small life will pass away. I would like to be as calm as space.

I imagine you to be that calm, Friend, wherever you are, out there on another planet, perhaps a planet of your own, like the Little Prince's, with only my letters to treasure, but all the Universe to know. You do treasure my letters, don't you?

Your Friend, Debbie

****

June
Dear Friend,

Debbie Bumstead

From my seat in the study, I could see a jumping spider hunting on the back of our couch in the living room. The spider turned this way and that as if looking at things, but it didn't know I was watching from several feet away. My thought gave me the most eerie feeling that I was being watched, too, by some being much advanced and in a totally different reality than mine. A spider, if it could know us, might consider us gods, since we could easily give them easy lives or smash them. So then the beings above us, we seem to consider gods because they could control our lives, if they chose to. But just as we are not gods, those beings above us are not gods - that's just the thought I had while watching the jumping spider going about its life on our sofa.

I watched a nature program about the chimp study done over many years by Jane Goodall and others. The chimps' lives affect me as I am affected by other animal lives that I either learn about through TV or books or which I know of personally. The world is so full of individuals and individual joys and loves and tragedies, and they are all going on right now at this moment in every single inch of the world. It is terrible on the heart to know.

Your Friend, Debbie

****

August
Dear Friend,

I like to see the little live bodies of children all naked and wet and round like baby seals. Their slicked down hair shines in the sun and their eyelashes stick together and they hold their arms close against their chests and run on tip-toe bare feet around the pool. The older children are taller, leaner; they are awkward, but move gracefully as they mount the diving board and jump or dive. My niece, Winter, likes to jump off the board, her nose plugged with two fingers She is tall and thin and brown with a bright bathing suit closing round her ribs and riding high on her boney haunches. Beau is broad-shouldered, handsome, suddenly deep-voiced, but wants to know, did I like to go off the board when I was young? He doesn't like to; he'd rather paddle around the deep end and watch the others. Spring makes friends in the shallow area, flops into the water, and screeches happily, as thin as her sister, but not as tall, and paler, more fragile. I swim around and splash and watch when they all call me to watch. I don't like to swim with my head under, so I do the sidestroke or paddle on my back, my eyes dreaming up at the blue sky and the thunderclouds crowding the edges of the mountains.

Your Friend, Debbie

****

September
Dear Friend,

I have a new friend next door, Rebecca, my brother Joe's live-in girlfriend's little daughter. Rebecca is short: "4'2" and 54 pounds," she tells me. She has blond hair that she forgets to comb before coming over to visit. "I forgot," she warns me, and she shakes her hair as if she were a puppy shaking its ears. She has bright blue eyes that search out mine as she tells me stories. "Can I tell you a story?" she asks. Then she hops up and down on the porch and twirls around the porch pole. "Well, once when I was a younger person," she tells me, "when I walked with my mom to get the mail, well, I stopped and said, 'there's a stone in my boot.' And we shook my boot out and looked and it wasn't a stone. So we looked on my heel and there was a tack stuck in it!"

Rebecca has a strong voice full of happiness and energy, but she is shy. She told me, "I want a best friend at school, but all the girls in class are paired off, except one, and she's no fun." I wish I could provide her with a best friend - I think I could be one myself, if only I were seven like she is.

Your Friend, Debbie

****

December

Dear Friend,

A couple of days ago I was sitting in the shop apartment with Rebecca and her mom, and Rebecca was opening the little windows on her Advent toy, a paper house her grandma had given her, and reading the Bible verses revealed.

"I don't like to read them," she said.

"Maybe you'll like the Bible when you're older," I said.

"I suppose," her mom remarked, "she might read it to know the culture."

"Maybe she'll even want to go to church when she's older."

"How many times have you gone to church in the past year?" Becky's mom asked me, implying that an adult wouldn't voluntarily choose to go to church.

"Four or five times," I said, and they opened their mouths in surprise. But that was last spring, and now I have as little faith as they do.

"I'm not a Christian." That's what I heard Rebecca telling the neighbor girl, when we were all playing together in the shop. The two children talked and I eavesdropped, my favorite thing to do around children. "I believe in Jesus and everything," Rebecca said, "but I'm not a Christian."

The word Christian reminds me of being thrown to the lions; that's my first thought on hearing the word. So it is with me, thrown into a pit, knowing I am trying my best and waiting for faith to well up and defeat the beasts. But it never does.

But I like the holiday, the Christmas tree, the ornaments, the feelings that the stories about Santa Claus and the Jesus child born to lead us into goodness give me.

Rebecca does believe in Santa, or at least she used to. She told me, "Santa is like God, you have to believe in him for him to be true, but he isn't really true. Is he?"

Christmas is here, anyway. This morning Phil and I hiked down to the motel loaded with my handmade presents, pillows and doodads that take months to make and one day to get rid of, but that's what Christmas is, too. When we entered Grandmother's apartment, a shiny new bicycle caught my eye and made me remember a Christmas morning when cousin Donna and I were eight and found shiny new pogo sticks under the tree. The bike was for Becky, of course. She acted as our Santa, handing presents lickety-split left and right until we all were buried in papers and ribbons and the opened gifts which seem to gleam especially brightly just after they are revealed.

**

The year is almost over. Why am I here, I wonder, and what am I to do with what I am given? I wanted to study the plants and animals of the world to see if their lives have the answer, but instead I have just been living along, working at school and around the house, talking to this person and that, reading a book or two and writing, remembering things, watching and suffering the weather, and so on.

I see the people I know as connectors in a large design, like nails on a board with colored yarns wrapped around them connecting them, Mama, Daddy, Grandmother, Joe, Tim, Phil right beside me, all my relatives, my friends, Debbie, Miss Kerr, all of them, Dr. Pullias, and further back in the design people I've known in the past but hardly know now like Mr. Hill and Dr. Eulert and Dr. Reid and scores of others who were important to me in their time. All these people are nails on the board of my design, and when one dies, like Grandpa or Grandbee or Linda or any others who have died, then their spots on the design dissolve into my memory. One by one I suppose they will all go, until at some point I go, too. Then what happens to my design? I feel like it will only be left here in the words I write.

I see you on your peaceful planet browsing over my previous letters, putting them together in order and perhaps finding some answer. It has something to do with observing the natural world, remembering the past, loving Phil and recalling our days together, knowing those people in my design, and something else that has to do with you, far away, up in the spirit world of my imagination. I know you understand me and wait patiently for my letters, dear friend that you are.

Your Friend, Debbie

❧Road Trip Memories ❧

One day in the year after Phil's death, I took Mama to her lab tests early, and then we went to Carrows for breakfast. After we ate, I waited on the bench outside while she went to the restroom, and I felt the dewy crisp morning air and heard the sparrows chirping. Immediately I thought of Phil and me traveling, starting out early, stopping in strange towns for breakfast, driving mile by mile, comrades of the road, sights seen and left behind, but most of all the joy of being enveloped in Phil's happiness of going on, escaping one place and discovering another. Sitting on the bench outside Carrows, the pain of it struck right into me -- how I wished he were there, and both of us well, able to travel again. A desperate thought came to me - Oh, my gosh, how great were moments in life never to come again to me.

***

Phil and I packed the Fiesta full of tent and mattress and everything else we needed for our vacation, and we drove away from Reno north to Washington. This was in the summer of 1990 just after Grandpa Marlow died. We went through the forests above Susanville to Mt. Shasta City and then up 5 to Medford. None of Phil's relatives were home there, so we went on to a small place beyond Grants Pass called Canyonville. We had a supper in a cafe and then set up our tent in a shady campground right by the highway.

Our spot was under a messy madrone tree above a green bushy ravine. We sat in our folding chairs awhile with nothing much to do. On our drive I had asked Phil if we could make love in the tent, so we were waiting for night-time to come for our fun. When it got just dark we went in to lie down together, and I giggled a little. I kept my voice low, but I could see over Phil's shoulder the tent canvas shaking, and it was embarrassing to know the other campers were still wandering around in the evening, while we were making love in our tent.

Maybe everyone knows the round togetherness feeling of traveling with the best beloved person in their lives. Side by side in the car is the perfect place to talk back and forth easily. Phil and I drove and drove on up through Oregon and then crossed the Columbia River bridge to Washington. As the iron girders flashed sunlight at us, I told Phil, "When I took a summer vacation from college in 1975, and my dad and I drove across this bridge, it seemed like magic. I actually felt the air turn to something more special, sweeter, greener, than of any other place I knew." And Phil replied and repeated throughout our trip, "I love the trees."

I remembered that time in '75 when our dad and I went to visit Joe, who lived with a girlfriend and her kids on Discovery Bay. I stayed with them a week surrounded by the most beautiful landscape - below the yard of wild roses, across marshy green stalks where herons fished, beyond turquoise waters with sun yellow reflections, grew the forest green forests, looking like a plush velvet fabric covering all the hills around. Now Phil and I were seeing those same trees, that same landscape.

But time had changed a lot, and driving on freeways overpowered the love of trees for awhile. When we reached Olympia, we were too tired to look for a campground, so we stayed in an expensive hotel. We didn't mean to, but we had passed the cheaper ones, and didn't feel like going back. The freeways confused us and made us even more tired, till we just took what came to us. But we made arrangements by the phone in our room to stay in a campground in Kent near Seattle for the following nights of our visit. Then we settled down and watched TV like old fogies.

I had a history with the state of Washington. I told Phil that when I was in second grade, we left California and lived for a year on the edge of a small bay near where we were in our hotel, in Olympia. "I was seven, Joe, 14, Tim 12. I don't know if every age has its impressions that stay with a person for the rest of their lives, but we three all still love the green forest state like it's a dream that we must attain again in some perfect future."

"I understand that!" Phil replied. "I would love for us to live here."

So I told Phil more, just because that is what he was to me so wonderfully - someone I was not afraid to talk to! I'd never had a person like that in my life! I was not afraid even of boring him! I could tell him about the summer, after graduating college, I went back to Washington with the goal of living there, getting a job, and becoming who I planned to be, a librarian perhaps, or a school worker of some kind. My dad had come up with me again and we hooked up with Joe again, too. I rented a house in Port Townsend near the ocean with my savings, but I couldn't find a job. I was so very lonely, and yet I didn't want my dad and brother to live with me like they were. "I wanted to be a grown-up," I told Phil. "I wish you had been with me then." Both of us often said this to each other through the years, that we wished we'd met earlier in life.

Our 1990 camp spot was not a typical Washington setting. There weren't any trees nearby, just flat land and a dike with a bike road running along it to our left. Behind, a grassy field held the campers who hadn't got spots with water like ours. Across the pavement from us was a German or Swedish family; all of them, man, woman, boy, girl, wore skimpy bathing suits as they puttered around trying to find things to do. I had to hike past four or five rows of campers to get to the restroom; in one spot a cat on a leash played in the grass.

Phil and I fixed our breakfasts and sandwiches for lunch and read the want ads to see how much houses cost to rent. There were some reasonable prices, cabins or houses in the country, $350 or $400. I felt like going to see one, renting it outright and just staying. Phil wanted to check on some colleges in Seattle, so we drove up the freeway and got lost in the big city. We also wanted to go up the Space Needle, but we couldn't find a parking place near it. Then we gave up on Seattle and tried to find a park which was supposed to be hidden in among the fancy houses along the Sound. But road repair blocked the park and we couldn't get in. We went back to our plain and dull campground.

I was disappointed. Phil asked me what I wanted to do, and I said, "I just want to get down to the water." So the next day we drove back to Seattle and onto the Winslow ferry. Now we were on the water. I felt better. Now we were free of traffic and maps and right and wrong turns. We could see; we had perspective, the expanse of water between us and the land. Seattle looked interesting as it faded into the distance. We were nearing an island that seemed overcrowded with trees instead of buildings. Houses stuck on the cliffs above the beaches made Phil and me jealous to live in them. Phil repeated as he drove around the island through the trees, "I love this kind of country. I don't often say that about a place, but I love this place."

He loved the trees and I loved the trees and the water. We had another ferry ride back from Bremerton to Seattle, a longer ride, through several turns past forested islands and peninsulas, with more homes among the trees to wish we had, and the water stretched out all around us, and the wind buffeted our hair as we stood at the bow. I remembered another ferry ride from one of my previous trips to Washington during which someone tried to fly a kite off the side. Funny thing to do, I told Phil.

Was that the year, I wondered, in 1983, that my childhood friend, Joan and I went on a road trip together, up into Washington to take a cruise-like ride on the ferry that went from the U.S. to Canada and back. That was a beautiful and fun trip, too, and Joan and I also camped out. In Reno before we left, I had hugged Phil goodbye in the dark outside my cottage, and I knew he was waiting for me to come home. He and I had just begun to hug and kiss, and I thought that soon we would make love. I recall that my body took hold of this possibility one moment as Joan drove us through the famous trees and down the ocean side of Washington; I suddenly became so aroused sexually, all quietly by myself in the passenger seat, that I would have burst if I'd been alone.

Now Phil and I took photos of ourselves, he with his curly hair in the wind, I with a bright Hawaiian shirt and shades flipped up from my glasses. We saw pretty colored sailboats out on the golden water and then Seattle again gradually coming into view. That was our last day. We thought about going to Port Townsend and looking up my old house, but I didn't really want to. We wandered through the small town of Kent in the evening and figured we'd come back and live there; though it was just a plain sort of town, the rents were good.

But we came home to Reno and didn't see Washington again for ten years. All that time we thought that someday we really did mean to go to live in Washington. Someday like in the song, "Someday, somehow, somewhere." Where? In Washington.

Those ten years later, after my Grandmother had died, Mama decided to sell the motel and land to the University.

My brothers wanted to go live in Washington, too. Then Phil's mom financed an airplane trip to Seattle for Phil and me and herself to scout out some property. We landed, scrambled onto an airport minibus, and were driven a wild ride through many freeways passing many wharves and factory places, everything gray colored and the traffic like a hive of a million bees. That night in the hotel up north of Seattle I cried and cried. How could my beautiful Washington be so full of cars and grey roads, all moving so fast? It was that first night that I decided I would stay in Reno, even if Mama and my brothers moved away. The next morning I told Phil and he gently accepted my news. Doris did, too, and we had a pleasant day going to a small town and eating at a canal-side café called something like Good Cat, Bad Cat.

We went back to Reno, which now seemed to be the inevitable thing to do. Mama bought my brothers a house and Phil and me a house with a mother-in-law apartment for herself, and so we lived in Reno. Now Phil has been gone seven years, my brother Tim even longer, my mom is 92 and Joe lives in his house one valley over from mine. Washington must go on without me as beautifully as ever, and I still wish I could see.

***

We talked, we were quiet, we listened to soft rock on the radio, we pointed out sights and daydreamed aloud on our numerous road trips. On one trip home, Phil and I started naming all the natural place names we could think of, such as: canyon, ravine, plain, field, hill, and so on. When we got into the more unusual words (gulch, peak, crevasse), I got out a notepad and began writing down all we came up with. It was lots of fun, and I still sometimes hear or think of another, while I drive now by myself

The very most delight I felt and my most spontaneous

laughs came from a funny game Phil and I had while driving in town, to sing made-up old country song blues. How the man lost his woman, or vice versa, how the trees were a'weepin', or the lonesome heart was a'bursting. One of us would make up and sing a few lines in a twangy country voice, and then we'd laugh and laugh. Then the other would create a few lines, and we'd laugh some more. It was so fun, I'm smiling right now. That is one memory that has no sadness to it, only longing.

***

Every year or two we took a trip to Hemet, my hometown in Southern California, to see my father who was living alone in the trailer on my mom's rocky hilly property, after the cabin burned down. Since middle age Daddy had had Huntington's Disease, an inherited disease of the brain that caused uncontrolled movements and emotional degeneration. He had once been a tall strong creatively intelligent man who built things of wood and philosophized about life; now he was crabbed up in body, and stubborn in mind, but he and I still enjoyed talking together, and Phil fit right in. I think the fact that they both smoked added a connection between them. I see them now, sitting in the lawn chairs under the billowy cottonwood tree, Daddy stuffing his pipe thoughtfully, Phil bringing out his pack of cigs and tapping it the way he did to get one out, and then the smoke fragrant of the two men I loved sifting into the air.

One year Phil and I drove to Hemet before Christmas through snowy Sierra mountains down into rainy California desert. Because my dad was staying in town with his second wife (it's a long story), Phil and I camped in the trailer at Red Hawk Hill. From there we made forays to visit my friends and my Aunt Rae and Daddy. Aunt Racheal gave me a long autobiography she had written, and I remember so well the cozy day it rained and rained and Phil and I stayed inside the tiny trailer, me on the bed reading Aunt Rae's life, and Phil calmly drawing at the table. Another moment so sweet!

Red Hawk Hill, the land my mom owned was right next door to the Sleepy Hollow land that my Bumstead grandparents had bought in the forties, where we grandchildren had hiked and played around their little adobe house through the 50s and 60s. All that joy and beauty of playing in nature was offset in my unconscious by Uncle Hersey's creepy presence and my swallowed up memories of him hurting me in the adobe home's bedroom and bathroom. He lived there now that my grandparents were gone, and one year during a summer when Phil and my brother Tim were working together cleaning up Red Hawk Hill of fire damage and Daddy's junk, Uncle Hersey haunted Phil, too. "I see him hiking every day on the dirt road up the hill above us," Phil told me on the phone, "like he's spying on us." During another phone call to me as I waited in Reno, Phil told me that as he slept in the tent he'd put up, while Tim was in the trailer, he woke and saw the silhouette of a man on the canvas of his tent, presumably my uncle just standing still outside. "Creeped me out," Phil said.

I guess it is best that we didn't follow the idea of building on Red Hawk Hill and living there after all. Phil and Tim had got tired of the hard work, and came home again. Despite my love of the Hemet hills, to live near the site of so many episodes of sexual abuse - not only to me but to other little children caught alone and hurt in an awful way by Uncle Hersey - and with the very man who had committed them as neighbor - might not have been so good.

To finish the history of Uncle Hersey, he kept all this pedophilia secret for years, and had once been considered the "good son" with his religious fervor, his steady work, his taking care of wife and five children, his whole fake life. But then finally he was caught abusing his granddaughter at

Sleepy Hollow - in the very way I remembered being abused - and that brought out the whole gross story. He confessed to lifelong abuse of relatives' and friends' children as well as children off the street, making sure they were under six or so, in order to prevent the acts being remembered and told of later. He was so adept at keeping his actions secret, while at the same time seeming as if he were a good man, that none of the adults caught on, none of the parents were able to protect their children. Later, when the little granddaughter's mother told me the story of her discovery of him, I was impressed with her quick action in calling in the police, and helping the truth come out. However, he wasn't imprisoned, and the mandatory counseling probably didn't stop him; only time stopped him. Like my dad, Uncle Hersey began to suffer from Huntington's Disease, and he soon died.

What all this has to do with my marriage to Phil is indefinably great: for without Phil I would not have healed as much as I did. As I've said before, Phil gave me the freedom to speak. I had been silent for 30 years, told by my uncle never to tell, which made me super quiet in all respects. But with Phil now, I could talk! I wasn't afraid to laugh and babble, gossip and philosophize, even yell once in awhile. Phil gave me the freedom to touch, too, which Uncle Hersey had stunted in me. For so long I had craved touch, but had hung back from hugs and kisses and sitting close and being sexual - until Phil tamed me. With Phil, at least, I was not shy, and for me, that was big. I only wish I had been able to speak up as a child or a young adult about Uncle Hersey, to somehow stop him earlier from hurting so many other fragile little humans.

The road trips to Hemet soon slowed, after our sick dad was brought up to Reno to be cared for. I missed the poppies blooming in the desert we saw one year on a spring visit, missed the smoggy smell of Hemet as we came over the hills of Beaumont, missed the warm strength of the boulders of Red

Hawk Hill, all sunned on top and shaded beneath, and I even missed the tiny details of flora, buttercups, wild buckwheat, and fauna, lizards of all colors, stinkbugs, rock wrens and more.

I remember on that visit we made in winter, on the way home to Reno, we came up out of the valley of Bishop into the foothills of the Sierra Mountains, and snow began to fall gently. The higher we climbed in our new little blue car, the heavier the snow fell. How silent it made the road and the traffic around us, and how scary the prospect of further driving in higher mountains. We stopped in Bridgeport and got the very last room in a motel on the highway. It was still early afternoon as we settled into the big corner room with windows on the scenic landscape of falling snow. Phil took a rest, while I turned on the TV. I watched a very favorite old show I'd liked as a teen, *The Avengers* with Patrick Macnee and Diana Rigg. I hadn't seen the show in years! So, we had a lovely stay, a mini vacation within the vacation. When we had eaten our meals of snacks, watched more TV, and then got into bed, I began to cry about a problem at work. I suppose I'd taken a vacation from worry, but then it came out, how one professor had complained about my not circulating enough amongst the students, and now I had to go back in a few days to face her. Phil held me close and told me I was better than any of them knew, the dopes.

Oh, how I loved my Phil, how safe he was, how strong, how warm, how healing he was to me! In the morning the sky was bright blue and the highway was packed with snow. We had chains put on the car and spent a beautiful drive through the mountains with other travelers in other cars on their own road trips, some on the way out and some, like us, going home.

❧Daydream Children ❧
1991- Memories

In 1991 times were difficult, so difficult that I didn't keep a journal, or if I did, I tossed it later and forgot it. I only have the five year diary entries to see what we both were going through individually and together. I spent many months in pain, menstrual pain that lasted three weeks out of each month. I tried out some pills that helped a little, but caused weight gain and also made my libido go up: testosterone. I remember the doctor asking me about that and then joking that he ought to get his wife to take the medicine, too. And I was thinking inside, if only my husband would appreciate my increased need.

Phil and I still held to his promise with sex once a week, but I had to remind him most times, and other times I had to beg him or cry stormily into my pillow several days before he relented. I guess his viewpoint was different, that he wasn't hurting me on purpose, but he didn't feel like making love. He took many medicines himself that reduced his libido! Maybe I was really quite lucky that he was manly enough to overcome the meds to please me. The best thing about Phil, even when he turned off the sex later in our marriage for some years (years!), was that he remained huggy, warm, and sweet with me as we struggled onward.

Debbie Bumstead

And meanwhile, as 1991 went on, he was depressed and becoming more disturbed as the days passed. Phil was only 48. He was physically fit from all the work he'd done at the furniture store in Gridley. Maybe that year's healthy living had squished down his disorder of the mind, and now it was hurrying back in the worst way to make him suffer. Or, it could have been, since I don't remember, the years when he was changing medicines and one didn't work and the other did but not enough and so on. For the first time in our marriage, Phil went to stay in a hospital, a VA Domiciliary in Pennsylvania where he was monitored and given therapy. He had gone there of his own accord, after a quest of some kind back east had not turned out, so he was able to leave when he wanted. A month later he came home and gave his mom and me some jewelry he had made in occupational therapy, pretty pendants on chains, which of course we both cherished.

Meanwhile I had an operation, in which it was found I had an ovarian cyst and endometriosis. When the cyst was removed, the doctor eagerly told me I could still have a baby, and that led to Phil getting his sperm tested. What a funny scene it was at home collecting it and then rushing down to the doctor's office. Phil's sperm were slowpokes, but the doctor again eagerly told us he could help us get pregnant with in vitro or some other way. Both of us wanted a child, but we had no funds to pay, and I believe we both had a inner drawing back from the idea because of what seemed to be poor genetics in each of us.

My daydreams since age 5 of seven children, or twins, or even just one boy or girl didn't die; they just became impossible. Here I am at sixty-one, and I still sometimes think about the child we might have had in 1991, how old would he or she be now, and how sweet our little family would have been, Phil and me and a child all loving each other. Phil liked the idea of having a boy, because, "then if he's plain like us, it won't matter as much as it would to a girl." The name Glenn, for Phil's kindly uncle, I said would be the boy's name, and if a girl maybe Shasta, for Mt. Shasta City, a tiny town in California. We often stayed the night there on our way to Oregon - I imagined that maybe that is where she would have been conceived.

Debbie Bumstead

⚘Hard Times & Gentle Pets ⚘
1992 - 1993 - Memories

1992 was the worst sick year I had known for myself, and Phil also remained troubled. He spent most of his time in Medford with his mom, or in the VA Domiciliary near there. Though we called each other almost daily, Phil was so down, he told me a couple of times that "My life is too hard to have a wife." But his spirits would rise a bit by the next day, and we stuck to loving each other. I guess you could say we loved each other unconditionally, considering the sadness that kept us apart.

The painful endometriosis built up again in me, and then I had to wait months for a surgery time. I had a hysterectomy, which solved all the cramping problems and other stuff that had been going on since I was 13. Later in psychotherapy, I learned that children who have traumatic experiences are more likely than others to have chronic pain and autoimmune diseases as adults. Apparently when a child, the genes that turn on flight or fight and then turn it off when it is safe, learn to stay turned on all the time, and that changes the body, makes it more apt to acquire fibromyalgia, for instance, which I'd had since age 32, and endometriosis.

As 1992 came to a close the nightmare of suffering before and after the operation kept repeating in my mind, as I tried to

94

recover with help from Mama and Grandmother. I only got worse, with pain remaining, then increasing in my abdomen. Back to emergency - now I had appendicitis! So two weeks after one operation I had another and spent a week in the hospital. When I came home, Phil was still gone, and my mind wouldn't quit telling itself the horror story of my illnesses over and over. Only when Phil finally came home, feeling better, ready to stay, did my oppression lift. Like a miracle, all gloomy thoughts ended, and I was glad again to be alive, with Phil.

I don't know how his mind's trouble worked, but he was better now, too. The rest of the nineties we were nearly constant companions. Though I worked, and sometimes he worked, we were together at home and going driving so often, I think maybe it is remarkable how pleasant and peaceful we were together.

***

One of Phil's childhood joys had been the animals he had: his duckling, his dog Spot - I heard lots of stories of Spot - and also a few chinchillas, which his dad once thought to breed and sell, one time a cow, and then the horses on the Montana ranch his uncles and mom owned, where Phil spent summers. But back in California as a boy, Phil made friends with a fellow who had pigeons, Birmingham Rollers, and gave a couple to Phil. Dad did not approve, so Phil hid his pets in their coop on a barn roof and loved their gentle ways, until Dad gave in.

My experience of pigeons was similar to most other people who don't know any birds personally; they were pretty in flight but pesty and poopy otherwise. But one day I found an ad for Free Birmingham Rollers, read it out to Phil, and we drove over to a regular house in a crowded neighborhood to look at a woman's backyard aviary. She gave us two pretty pigeons and an old rabbit hutch to make into a coop. Phil named the birds Snow and Inky, one was bright white and the other a pinto-colored bird, and they set up household on our front lawn in the hutch, and raised two babies.

Time passed, and we let the pigeons out to fly often, and up they would go, like tiny sailboats on the sea of sky. They did roll at times, somersaulting backward in the air over and over, and then swoop! Up they'd fly again. One day two men from the University came by in their truck. "We've been seeing your pigeons flying and decided to follow them, and see if you would sell some to us," they said. Phil, without consulting me, told the men to take all the pigeons with them; they could have them. I was sad to see the little pets go, since watching their lives together, I'd become attached.

Later, in the 2000s, as we were settling in our new house after the motel property sold, we sent away for some Roller pigeons who came in the mail. My brother Joe had fixed up a big coop in our country backyard, and from the first four, we soon had 20 pigeons, living their funny gossipy lives in the coop and flying out by day for a few hours to enjoy freedom. Phil liked them, but I fell in love. They were gentle to catch and pet, and I liked sitting in the roomy coop to watch their interactions - taking baths, building nests, making sure their wives or husbands were loyal, and fussing sometimes with the pecking order. I began to write down their stories, which I called Pigeon Gossip, to entertain my online book club friends, and soon had an article published in the magazine, *Pet Folio*.

It was in the 90s and the 00s that I took up writing articles, and many were actually published. For instance, because I'd been inventorying and researching Grandmother's large collection of 50s, 60s, and 70s dolls in order to sell them online, I gathered enough knowledge about them to write short pieces, such as *Grandmother's Wonderful Doll Collection, Dolls of the Stars of the 70s, Ethel the WPA Doll*, and more, which sold to several national doll magazines. I actually got paid for these!

Pet Folio also took an article about a basenji dog we rescued, but could not keep, do to his mischievous character and cat chasing habits. But back to 1992, about the time Holly, our old dog of 15, died, I wanted a new pet, too, since Phil had gotten his Boston, Bridget, and the first pigeons.

I dreamed one night that I ran across a green pasture, shouting, "Tugger! Tugger!" to a beautiful black German Shepherd dog. Dream Tugger was the dog I set out to find.

Phil took me to see an accidental litter - the woman's fine high-strung black shepherd had mated with a friendly homey old shepherd - there were like 12 puppies. I chose the one that was blackest (he still had sable legs and muzzle), the fuzzy one who went up to Phil and pulled his shoelaces. Tugger came home to join bubbly Bridget the pup, and Monty and Pie, the elderly cats. As I mentioned before - as Phil was the genius man, so Tugger was the genius dog. He was housebroken in one day, and lived his 12 year life being himself in an independent, yet loving, way that I'd not known in a dog before. My best previous dog, Rex, who had hung on my every word, even he was not as much himself as wise Tugger was.

Debbie Bumstead

⅄

❧Walk on the Sand for Me ❧
1994 - Memories and Journal Entries

Phil got a phone call one evening from his younger brother, Mark, that made Phil cry. Mark said that the doctor had tested a big mole on his leg and found it was melanoma.

As time went on we followed Mark's progress. The cancer had spread to his lymph nodes. He was to have a big chunk cut out of his leg and then other operations on the nodes. He went to have an experimental treatment in California. The whole family felt positive that he was going to get well. Phil drove up to visit him a couple of times in 1994, while I stayed home to work. Everyone still said he was getting well. I believed them, until I saw him myself, in June when Phil and I went up to Oregon for a vacation and to visit.

Mark, ten years younger than Phil, was the baby that everyone dotes on, who came way after the group of siblings before him. Phil loved his baby brother so much I want to cry about it right now. The first time I met Mark was at a college basketball game here in Reno where Mark's team was playing away. Mark was acting as substitute coach; he had once been a teacher and coach, but now owned a furniture store in Medford.

Phil's other family members came to watch; it felt funny to

sit on the other team's side for a change. Then Mark walked out on the floor, and I exclaimed to Phil, "He walks just like you do!" Later, after the game, when we all met down in the hallway, I saw that Mark was a good 6 inches taller than my tall 6'1" Phil. I also saw, or sensed, that though Phil still looked on his baby brother as a kid, Mark had taken on the role of - I don't know what to call it - caregiver, maybe, to Phil. This was the role that all of Phil's family took with Phil, except maybe his mom.

It couldn't be helped, really. Phil did need care, you could see it, if you knew him long enough. But this patronizing edge to their talks with Phil, hurt Phil sometimes. I was a little different; I looked on Phil as a wise, strong, intelligent, sexual man, and saw his many mental downturns as just something to suffer through. And meanwhile, Phil knew by heart all my own personal sufferings as well, so he felt he was caring for me. I believe this is how he felt about his mom, too.

Mark had a shy beautiful little wife and two boys going into high school. That first time I sensed Mark's tone, which made me a tiny bit resentful for Phil, soon changed to real love for Mark. When Phil and I moved to Medford that year of 1987, Mark became Phil's best friend. We often visited the family at their house, and we had loads of fun going to the boys' basketball games. Mark went out to lunch alone with Phil every other week or so. I remember one time Phil came home from a lunch out and told me Mark had asked how his sex life was, and Phil had told Mark, "She wants it even more than I do," to which Mark replied, "You are lucky." I was glad they talked together like that - maybe it would show Phil how lucky indeed he was!

And that year in 1987 had cemented my love for both Mark and his family, and now, in 1994, Phil and I were on the road north to visit them, as were many other family members, as death called.

Debbie Bumstead

From my Journal: June 7, 1994 - In Medford, Oregon

Yesterday we went to see Mark. I watched from the bedroom doorway as Phil helped Mark from his chair to his bed. Mark looked like a concentration camp survivor - dreadfully thin, gray in color, too weak even to speak very much.

As he sat at the side of his bed, he said, "I want to see Phil and Debbie." So Phil and I stood beside him. Mark raised his hand to take mine. I told him I loved him. He said he loved me. He said he had had a bad morning, referring to his passing out in his wife's arms in the shower. He said, "Today's a good day for sleeping."

When we left and got into the car, I began to cry. It was a shock to see him so weak when I've been used to seeing him so strong. I see how close to death he is, though many in the family still think he will get well. The cancer, starting from a mole on his leg and spreading through his body, seems to me an insidious evil the way it has slowly consumed a healthy energetic man in the prime of life.

Today we saw Mark twice. In the early afternoon he told us he was better today. He said, "I turned a couple of corners today."

I told him, "I think you're a great person," and he said, "I think you're a great girl." Phil took his younger brother's hand and touched his hair. Mark's eyes slipped shut as he fell asleep.

Later we went again. This time he talked more to us. He said, "I heard you are going to the Coast tomorrow" Then, "God gave us this world to enjoy the beautiful places." And, "Walk on the sand for me."

A few weeks ago when Mark was in the hospital getting treatments, Phil went to visit him, and he said to Phil, "If Phil could find a way, he would make me well."

June 16, 1994 - Wednesday

"Oh, My Redwood Heart!"

It is early morning in Medford, the day after Mark's funeral. Today Phil and I are going home to Reno. Last Wednesday we drove from here to Coos Bay through forest land. When we got there we were led by signs to Sunset Bay, a small cove in the trees. We got out of the car and walked across the sand. Phil sat on a rock, while I took off my shoes and socks and walked along the water. Three children played in the shallow waves and filled the air with shouts and laughter. The waves came in, rippling over my feet. I felt happy.

Then we found a motel room and then drove north of Coos Bay to the Dunes National Park. We drove along a road through scrub pine trees, not knowing where we were or if we would ever reach the ocean. We came to a large parking lot with a grassy ridge along one side. We walked over that hump and saw, heard, smelled, tasted, felt the mighty ocean. The beach stretched flat a long way up and down and small figures of couples each seemed to have a portion of beach to themselves.

Phil and I walked on the sand for Mark. We wrote his name in the sand. We sat on a stump and looked far away across the water and at the white caps of the waves coming in lines along the beach. When the rhythmic roar of the ocean fills my ears I feel all's right in the world. I wished I could live on the beach.

We drove back to Medford the next morning and found Mark was going into the hospital because his breathing hurt his chest. We hurried over and joined the family group in the hospice waiting room. Pair by pair we went to visit in Mark's room down the hall. When Phil and I peeked around the curtain, Mark saw us and made a noise.

"Rest," his wife said, "rest." So we left without telling him we walked on the sand for him. The doctor put a morphine drip into Mark to ease his pain and anxiety. Then he slipped by degrees into death. First he moaned heart-rendingly with every breath he let out. Two hours later the moaning was softer. Later it stopped and he breathed quietly. Everybody - his mother, siblings, wife, sons, all the family and many friends from church and business, gathered in the darkened room as Mark's breathing grew slower and slower. Then he passed away.

***

At home again in Reno, I listened to the cassette of Lloyd Webber hits, and it seemed to me the playful Starlight Express expressed just how playful Mark had been to Phil and me, and I cried whenever I heard it, especially the words, "I don't want you to go...". Mostly I cried for Mark's wife because I kept thinking of her all alone, just as I might be if Phil died. I cried for her grief, never knowing my future - strange to think. I shared Phil's grief for his brother, too, some time after Mark's death, when my own brother, Tim, died of Huntington's Disease. I chose a song for Tim, too, one which Tim had liked when we were teens in the 60s, Herman's Hermit's *There's a Kind of Hush*. Before that, a long time ago, way before Daddy died, I'd picked my dad's song of a dreamer's life - *Somewhere* from *West Side Story*.

Then Phil's sister and her husband gave us a job for the summer, cleaning their furniture store in Fallon on Sundays. Oh, how I remember those Sundays with fond affection - how we worked together amongst all the shiny tables and chairs, sofas and beds, Phil vacuuming, me dusting and resting - I just loved to see Phil work! For then he became strong and efficient, physical, firm, focused, while I could take the lesser role, the weaker one who didn't have to pay attention.

I was almost always on high alert, paying attention to many details and making sure things were done, including Phil's stuff, like appointments and taking his meds. He sat doodling his ideas or artwork or slept or fussed with phoning about his businesses, while I got things done, or talked him up enough to do what he needed to do. One time he teased me, called me, "Mrs. Fix-it" because I was better at fixing problems around the house than he was. I loved the sedentary intellectual part of Phil, though, too, because he was the man who listened to my stories, let me talk as much as I wanted, while he listened and commented gently, wisely. Yes, those two Phils I loved dearly; it was the Phil who left me that I didn't like. In fact, I can remember saying to him, as he planned another trip after giving up the Fallon job, "Sometimes I hate you." I could say that to Phil, that's how safe he was, for he replied, "I know, sometimes I do, too."

That was 1994, the year Mark was sick and died, the year Phil and I worked in Fallon, the year Phil went off for two months to live in Medford again, the year I went back to work at the college and waited for him to come home. That was the year we walked on the sand for Mark.

❧Two Letters ❧
1994 & 1995

Letter from me in Reno to Phil in Medford, Oregon, 1994
Dear Phil,

Sorry I hung up on you. Guess I'll let you call sometimes so I don't feel like I'm interrupting you all the time. It's so cruel to be apart. I'm lonely every afternoon, so it feels like my lonely time before we got married - <u>years</u> of loneliness. All of that disappeared when we came together, so I hate to see it back again. Our lives are too short to be apart, but that's what you've chosen.

At work I was given all last semester's tests to redo for this semester. I have to do Chapter One by Monday or Tuesday. I brought them home and so far I've worked 40 minutes on them. Monday I'll take my corrections and type the test at the computer center.

I sent a letter to the publisher in San Francisco about seeing my Minikin books and the dragon book. I also could send them *Alice* and the child. lit. book. But first I'm asking the UNR press if they will look at *Alice*. Jeany suggested all this, so I was inspired to do it.

Tomorrow is Sunday and I plan to do all my laundry and also wash the car. My work schedule will be Monday and Tuesday: paperwork. Wednesday: in class 8 - 10:45. Thursday 8 - 3:15. I hope I can last through Thursday, but since my last two classes are with Ed I can be pretty relaxed. I don't have to walk around too much in his classes.

My mother ordered some blouses and things for me. I wish they would come. I have just two outfits for work. Kinda sad.

Why don't you come home for awhile when your mom visits at Fallon and stay till the 12th. Six days.

Love, Debbie

**

Letter to me in Reno from Phil at the Belmont Hotel, Okmulgee, OK - 1995

Dear Debbie,

My heart is always open for you. You called me a while ago and were hurt. I know its hard but what could be better than the two of us on our own and happy after I finish school. We will have enough saved to start our businesses any where. I'm thinking Ashland or Calgary. I want to assure you that every thing is going to be all right. Don't worry!

I worry about catching aids from my shower. What if an aids patient had athletes feet. Also there is a point on it and its chipped in places where aids might be hiding. I guess its okay.

My game is waiting till school starts to get an artist there to do the pictures. Its going to be real nice and different than games usually are. Its almost as good as the Interpreter is. If it's going to go we could get a house and start a business.

Love, Phil

⭑OK in OK, OK ⭑
1995 Onward Memories

Things quietly began to change. It was my last semester at the college; I was just too achy to do a good job. Instead I began selling things online, one by one the treasures my grandmother, my mom, and I had accumulated, books and dolls mostly. I sewed a lot of rag dolls, thinking I might make some money selling them, but I never did. I wrote - I began a book called *The Lonely Phonograph of Oz* to enter the big new Oz book contest to be held in 2000, the 100th anniversary of the Wizard of Oz - I received the manuscript back in 2001 with a sad little note from one of the judges: "I wanted your book to win."

Phil worked on a game he called Commerce in '95. I can't remember how it was played, but in my five year diary I often wrote that, "we played Phil's game." Now that Phil's mom was living near, we had her to visit, and I was thankful Phil no longer needed to go stay with her in Oregon. I believe her visits made Phil feel stronger, more like the person, the man, he wanted to be, as he took us on little adventures around town or to the forests in the mountains.

***

In early April, Phil and I drove down to Hemet for an adventure on our own. This was the time we made up funny car names. Phil thought of "Drama" and "The Great White." I thought of "Lava" and "Cheetah." Phil liked two big ranches we passed outside Minden. Lots of rowboats, each with one person in them, were scattered across Lake Topaz. We stopped in Walker and had hotcakes in a cafe that had used books in the front walkway for 50 cents each. In Bishop we rented a room and then drove around town looking at the homes.

Oh, my goodness, how can it be that I remember so realistically in my mind, almost as if it happened yesterday, looking at the paperbacks in the lobby of the café, and thought how appealing to find books for sale for just two quarters. And then how we chanced on the perfect plain and simple motel in Bishop. I can remember the room's blue walls, the window in the bathroom that gave a view of a field of the sandy earth, sagebrush and cottonwoods, so quiet compared to the street in front. The sensation of being with Phil is so heart-rending to me right this minute! It wasn't that he was always his best on our travels, but he was perhaps his happiest, with no goal to trouble him, other than getting there.

The next day, April 13, we drove through the desert - the brush was green, and the ground was covered with yellow wildflowers. The sides of the road had purple flowers and a few Indian paintbrush plants and buttercups nodding in the wind. In Hemet on the hill we met up with Daddy and he told us where to meet him for supper, at the Winchester Inn because he could both eat and smoke there at the bar. He looked fairly neat in brown pullover and jeans and cap, but he was skinny and crippled and slow-talking.

At the bar my dad told us this story: He parked his truck up on the hill under the cottonwood tree one night and sat in the cab drinking his "Southern Comfort." He fell asleep and must have hit the gearshift out of place because the truck rolled down the brushy rocky hill and he woke up the next morning sixty feet down in the truck wedged between two rocks. He had to crawl out of the window and get a tow truck guy to help him pull the truck up again.

Debbie Bumstead

The next day I spent with a good old high school friend; we watched movies at her house amid her four cats, Bubba, O.J., Buster, and Peaches. O.J. the cat had been named long before OJ Simpson became infamous, but it was that year, later in 1995, that we obsessively watched his murder trial

Sunday in the afternoon Phil and I went to see "Forrest Gump" which made both of us cry, and later we found Daddy sitting in his truck at the donut shop and asked him to come to the motel room. There we sat and talked until about ten. Daddy told us this: That he was spoiled and if he let himself be taken care of he just fell apart. He had let himself be taken care of in the past, but now he resisted everyone who felt he was helpless and needed a hand. I thought he was being a little mean by blaming others for his own spoiled state of the past, a little selfish. It hurt me, but I let it go. He was such a lonely shrunken up little person, but he was getting along as best he could. I was glad we had the visit there in the motel room for I had come down to Hemet especially to see him.

Phil was obliging on this trip, helping me do the things I wanted, like visiting my old San Diego college roommate, Debbie SZ, who I thought of as my other best person to love. So on that Monday I was sitting in the sun on the lounge by the pool outside our motel room in Oceanside when Debbie came walking by to pick me up for a day's visit. She and I drove around doing errands and talking cheerfully - I always had the nicest times with Debbie, she talked so easily with shy me. But though I loved her so, I could not be as free with her as I was with Phil. She could not seem to tame me.

When I joined Phil again, he and I went to sit on the rocks above the beach to watch the ocean. The sun descended through clouds, the waves broke rhythmically, a little terrier chased the sandpipers. I picked up a green stone, a red one, and a white one, too.

When we left Oceanside, it was raining fast and thick. We could hardly see on the rushing freeways; I got more scared as we went along, till I wanted to pull off and wait for the rain to pass. But brave strong, ex-truck driver (one year) Phil kept going. After we reached Riverside the rain stopped and we drove up to Bishop in peace. The next morning in the motel room we heard about the bombing in Oklahoma City. More of it was on the TV in the Denny's in Minden where we stopped to eat breakfast. We didn't know the bombing was so big and horrible until we got home and learned all the details.

***

Okmulgee, say that word three times real fast. It was a town in Oklahoma that had a school with a special jewelry course, which Phil wanted to take. I don't know how he found the places he went to, maybe in the college catalogs at the library, or maybe from people he talked to while pursuing his ideas. But there it was, Okmulgee, seeming to Phil the answer to his desperate need to do something for a living, in order to finance his great ideas and take care of me. It involved going away from me, but he never seemed to see that going away from me was the opposite of taking care of me, in my opinion. But in May 1995 he went to Okmulgee and rented a studio to live in, to wait for school to start.

Just as he and I had loafed around before my librarian course began in Oregon, Phil loafed around Okmulgee for a month. His room was near the post office, so for once he began to write me letters. Letter after letter came to me, and I liked seeing the thick long envelopes resting in the motel mailbox that I checked each day. We also called on the phone frequently. It is strange to me now, thinking about how connected we were, maybe too much so? I don't know. In my five-year diary I noted down that Phil was OK in OK,OK, but I wasn't OK in Reno.

Though he only stayed there a month, coming back as soon as he realized he actually had to go to school to attain his dream (as I had), I missed him very badly this time. His letters described the little town, his room, his walking to and fro - and I wanted to be with him. What was I doing anyway? It was beautiful early summer in Reno. I wrote, took care of household stuff, shopped with my mom, and often visited with six year old Rebecca, who was a big part of both Phil's and my daily life in the early 90s when her mom and my brother lived next door to us. Rebecca would hop and bop over to our house to talk or play, and neither Phil nor I ever tired of her, she was so young, so lively, cheery, and growing.

I liked the way Phil was with the children we knew, mostly my two nieces, Winter and Spring, Tim's daughters who came to stay a day and overnight through the 80s, and now Becky. He spoke to them gently. I used to wish he would play more with us, but he preferred to work at the table or sit nearby listening, being the grown-up he was, while I played the child for joy. Once we were visited by the adopted son of a church friend of my Grandmother's - Theodore, I believe the little boy's name was. Theodore (not Theo) was about six and the most talkative kid I'd ever met. Phil and I sat on our front porch, while Theodore skipped around and up and down and told us a great multitude of things. We laughed with him, and when he left, we laughed again, just at his garrulousness; Phil was charmed, since as he said, he'd been a talkative boy also, and we thought together about adopting such a child.

But with Phil gone now, even the children wouldn't do; I wanted Phil to come home from Okmulgee. Our nightly phone calls always ended in my tears, and his letters made me yearn to be with him. His letter about AIDS possibly lying latent in the shower stall didn't worry me; I recognized that Phil's worry was not reality, but a part of his illness. It disturbed me to see it in him, and now I wonder what other small delusions stopped his life from being what it could have been. Maybe there was a story in his mind about each job that he took on, and then had to quit within a short time. He said he didn't know why he quit, but maybe he did have a story that he knew I wouldn't believe, so he kept it from me. What a mix he was of intelligent self-awareness and crazed bits of non-reality! Sometimes if he seemed off in another world, unable to be present, I might say his name a few times, and in a blink, he resumed his healthy outlook and attention, and during that time, he could actually see some of his mistakes as mistakes. But not always.

Then, in June, I guess he did see reality, and he came home to me.

***

Just in time for the Miniature Horse Show at the Livestock Center. One of Phil's dream books was a picture book about the tiny horses, which we had bought when visiting a mini horse farm in the Napa Valley a year or so before. Once in awhile Phil dreamed of having a ranch, raising the little horses, and making lots of money. I liked this dream of his because I got to dream about naming animals. I liked making lists of names; this time I copied down many of the names of the characters in L. Frank Baum's Oz books, such as TikTok, Tin Man, Wizard, Miss Cuttenclip, and so on.

As luck would have it, the U.S. Mini horse Association held its yearly show two or three times in Reno. If Phil was daydreaming horses, then he was eager to go, and so came another of my favorite moments never to be known again to me. During the confirmation classes, Phil and I would pick our favorite to win, and Phil nearly always chose the actual winner, which impressed me, and which made him feel impressive. I loved to watch the freedom class, in which each single horse was let free for several minutes into the big arena, and the handler sought to make the horse cavort and gallop in the wildest or most attractive way possible. Sitting in the stadium watching and clapping, I adored the tidy, springy, little horses, so shining and prancing, I wanted to let them into my heart to live in a pretty pasture where I could always have them for my own.

Phil had several dream books. One was a catalog for log houses with lots of different floor plans. Another was a book of home plans, more traditional - Phil liked the Tudor style. He also had an old Sunset book of 50s houses that were sleek and desert landscaped. I liked Phil to settle down with a dream book. He was calm for hours, and we both could pretend out the future. My dream books were dog or cat breed volumes, or one of my many scrapbooks of cut out magazine photos of house interiors, animals, artwork, clothes, and so on. Does everyone have dream books? They are good for relaxing, sort of like meditating on the good that may come to you. And the good was coming to Phil and me, slowly, unfortunately accompanied by a lot of suffering, and then death. Is that how life works?

❧This World of My Heart ❧
The 90s in Selected Journal Entries

1992

When the clouds broke at about eleven, I sat where the sun comes through the glass door and saturates the couch. I can hardly move from that spot when the sun is shining, I seem so to crave sunshine and warmth. I'm studying a book called *Plot*. Phil didn't feel well today and so he slept. When he got up at 3 we readied ourselves for a date out - it is January 4th, our seventh anniversary. I put on my red-colored jeans, a white blouse under a bulky pink sweater, brushed my hair, wore my mocs. Phil wore his brown slacks and a plaid shirt that's getting faded around his big milk belly. He has quite a collection of shoes and socks given him by his mom after his dad died. We drove down the freeway in our turquoise Geo called "Dewdrop," turned off at Moana, cut across to Virginia and went up to the Sizzler across from the Peppermill Casino.

Phil had steak and lobster; I had giant fried shrimp. It took our food a long time to get to us, and then it was gone into our stomachs in a twinkling. It wasn't dark yet as we drove on home, up through downtown, past the casinos and their big signs announcing shows, with me thinking of the bright lights, strange life, strange world.

At home we listened to a scratchy radio program that had

some singers singing from Gershwin's "Porgy and Bess." Just as he used to the first year of our being together, Phil sang out the lyrics to one of the songs, "Ain't Misbehavin'" - about no one to talk or walk with, but he's happy; he ain't misbehavin' - he's saving his love for me.

***

Phil's sadness is going on and on. He takes his medicine and goes to bed early after puttering around all day doing not much. I'm not angry, but very concerned. I sat on the edge of the bed and tried to talk him into going to the hospital, maybe a mental health program would help him or a change in medicine. He says he can't be helped. He gets mad at me for thinking he can be helped or that he can at least try to be helped. But then he said, "If you weren't with me, I'd be in some room somewhere and no one would know or care."

I shouldn't be writing this down; Phil hates for people to know his problems. He has had these times of sadness going far back in his life, he tells me.

1993

Our 8th anniversary isn't until tomorrow, but Phil and I celebrated it today. After we drove Mama to work at Helen's, we stopped at Marie Calendar's and had brunch - waffles and bacon and sausage and little pies in individual tins. It was pleasant, something different. Afterwards we drove to the Indian colony for Phil's cigarettes, and then home. I'll tell you how nice the day was, just by saying we lay down to rest late in the afternoon, hugged close and began to kiss. Phil growled in a friendly way and made a suggestion. Quickly we whipped off our clothes - I had on several layers due to below freezing weather all the day - and hurried under the covers. Then followed the warmth and excitement of love between two who love one another, special even after eight years of marriage. We showered, went to pick up Mama, came back and watched the last half of **Dr. Zhivago** on TV. And the day went on...

***

There's a place with tall rickety wooden houses leaning over a paved, no, a cobblestone, lane, and up and down the lane walk violin players and lovers and graceful young horses loose from the meadow. And I'm up in a garret sitting at a window. I can see it all, the sky, the far forest, the lovers; as darkness falls, the stars appear, and I know my own love encompasses this world of my heart. And all the while the music - "Was it too beautiful to last?"

***

Today Phil told me he wanted to call me Little Bird instead of Little Flower. I said call me Sparrow. Like a sparrow I'm plain and one of many in this world. But I can sing and hop and fly and I can look around at the world with my bright round eye.

***

I received a call from Jeany at work who very kindly told me there's been some criticism of my shyness as a writing lab tutor - I wasn't interactive enough. Jeany was so sympathetic about it, asking me if I'd mind not being in the lab that I began to cry. I had thought I was a good tutor. I had to ask her to call back later. Then Phil held me and said I should be laughing instead of crying - I'm shy and that's all there is to it.

***

Here's a poem Phil said last night before he left for Fallon for his job guarding the tent sale at his family's furniture store. I call it:

> The Night Guard's Poem
> It is good --
> When dawn comes --
> the lightening --
> Night's shadows disappear
> And many ghosts fly away.

***

I hear voices from next door, the pigeons cooing, a cricket. I plan to start a new mystery, also to watch TV, a program on the pyramids, and the X Files. Phil is next to me here on the couch. We are a pair.

***

All last night thunder boomed and lightning lit up the room, hail clattered and rain pattered. I didn't sleep much and poor Bridget was miserable. She hates the thunder.

At work I didn't feel well. I had a headache and my muscles in my back hurt. Ed had a lecture thing going, so he told me to go on home.

In the afternoon, after we drove Mama to her new part-time job (helping change an invalid's bed) and back (since her car broke down), Phil and I settled down in the living room with our books and letters and animals and news. Phil put on his slippers and I put on my warm sweatsuit and the rain fell outside and the animals played quietly on the rug.

***

A day off finally. I spent it resting mostly. I did my

laundry and I cleaned the pigeon cage for Phil (pulling out all the soiled chips and spreading new in the three little bachelor apartments) and I walked to 7/11 for a paper and I worked on my paper mache, but mostly I rested. Phil finished reading his book, *The Tall Stranger*, and later told me a story about our made-up wild horse band. We were sitting on the bed with the cats and dogs around us and I asked what Rough n Tumble was up to with his pals TopsyTurvy and Rolypoly. PeanutButterBrickle and Steeldust had a filly named Pal. I-Told-You-So, the stallion, scared off some rustlers, and the whole herd outran the Indians, even when the Indians used rally ponies.

1995

I got up and was cold, so I took a blanket into the living room. I turned on the TV to watch the Saturday morning horror flick, which today was titled *Robot Monster*, one of those dumb fifties films that I love to see. Phil had eaten my half of a banana, so I went to the bedside with my hands on my hips to tell him that I had cut the banana and put his half on the microwave, and then placed my half on my cereal box so that he would know it was mine when he had his midnight snack, and couldn't he figure that out? But he had eaten them both. I teased him about it a couple of times today.

***

Thursday Phil turned 53. Today we took a drive to Galena Park, our favorite place to go close by. It is across Reno and up Mt. Rose Highway, the second entrance where the creek runs. We ate our peanut butter and jelly sandwiches, drank our Snapples, and sat on the bench near the creek. I walked alone up the path to the bridge. The path was covered with bright yellow leaves. I leaned against a boulder and looked downstream, at the water roiling over stones, at the pines and the cottonwoods nearly bare; I looked all around, feeling pleasure at the sights. A tiny spider wafted in the air beside me and a gnat flew by. The sky was cloudy, the air cool, and through the branches I saw Phil sitting alone on the bench. I thought of how as a teenager I used to be so impressed with my occasional opportunities to be alone in nature. I used to go off alone to hike. I was so often alone. But now I am a middle-aged person and down the path sat my husband. I never had any inkling then of the reality of having a husband and not being alone; that was all a daydream to me. I walked down the path again and sat close to Phil.

***

Phil and I drove to the 7/11 and I bought a peach Snapple for him and a Ben and Jerry's New York Crunch ice cream bar for me. We crossed to the park and sat in the car overlooking the fall-colored trees. I ate my ice cream bar slowly, savoring it and thinking I might as well enjoy something today, it has been such a low sort of day. We saw some people coming up the walkway of the trail through the trees; one was an older woman with a headset on that had an antenna, and I said, "She is an alien with antennae," and Phil said, "Many worlds are existing on ours."

***

Last night it began to blow and then to rain. The power went out. Phil and I had been talking on the couch, so we continued in the dark, after we had found our twin flashlights. We talked about miniature horses, trout farms, doll shops, book shops. We talked about Phil's game, real estate, weaving, and ceramics. We discussed my proposed activities: being in the Oz Club and the dog obedience club and volunteering an hour a day at an elementary school. We talked about the book I'm reading called *How to Want What You Have*. We put bowls under the leaks in the ceiling, and we went outside on the porch with the dogs to watch the rain and smell the sweet sage and rabbit brush. The darkness was shiny with rain. It hasn't rained in Reno for a record 100 something days, but last night it rained.

***

Yesterday evening I put on some music and went in to sit with Phil who was lying on the bed. I rubbed my fingers through his hair as we listened to "Starlight Express."

"Hear the harmonica?" I said. "I might learn the harmonica. It might be easy."

"The harmonica is easy. I can play it," Phil said.

"That song?"

"Maybe not that song."

"Starlight Express reminds me of Mark, I don't know why," I said. I sort of know why: first I just got the cassette last year around the time he died and second it is a playful song sort of like he was to me, and third because of the words at the end of the chorus, "I don't want you to go..."

We listened to the music and I felt sad about Mark, and about Phil's daydreams that never come near true. When the Requiem song played, I felt sad about all the striving of the world, how people created their religions to give them solace from the truth of death. It is such a sad and beautiful effort to make life worthwhile, but it doesn't work, only makes the world divided. Those who want a better life after death have heaven, and those who want a better life than the one they have now have reincarnation. All the religions seem to have one answer or another depending on what question is most important to them. Because of that it seems obvious to me that the religions are all made up for our own benefits. I feel sad about it, that we've all been fooled by ourselves since our time began because of our fear of death. We can't help it; we are such thinking beings. Even I am trying to think it all out to answer my own question.

1996
Phil's so loving and friendly. And the day is so beautiful to look upon.

***

Except today Phil kept on about moving somewhere new and his talk hurt me, so I'm terribly sad. I wandered around outside in the light rain feeling blue. I picked some sweet peas for the vase. I left Phil to himself in the living room and cried awhile in the bedroom. He changed his mind about going to Alaska; now it's Sacramento. But he'll go there and not make it and come back and then say he can make it in Alaska after all or somewhere else. He never wants to stay right here. Will he ever give it up, that idea that someplace else he'll be able to work, move me to him, and be well? I just have to bear it year after year, two, three times a year -- his going away and coming back, his constant yearning to leave and be someone else. I have that yearning, too, but I don't act on it anymore. When will he give it up and be happy here? In order to cope with his talk of leaving, I have to shut it out which hurts his feelings. He thinks I should encourage him to leave!
Sometimes I feel like leaving first. But I know that's impossible.

***

Phil and I started out today to go to the grocery store, but as we neared the Bonanza Casino, I asked if we could stop and have pancakes. As we walked into the casino, I smelled that cigarette liquor old carpet human smell of casinos and heard the slot machine chinking clinking sounds and saw the darkness lit by colored lights flashing numbers and pictures, but especially the smell, I think, effects me. I felt that exciting slightly hurting feeling of romance. All because when Phil and I were romancing, we often went to casinos for meals. We'd sit in a booth, Phil smoking, me pushing the silverware around, talking about ourselves, and me always wondering was it happening, was I really in love and being loved back? I like to go into casinos now and feel that feeling. It renews my love for Phil, helps me to remember how he gave to me the real love that I craved and needed so badly.

***

I'm mad at Phil, and it hurts me to be. I ask him to help with the housework; his job is to vacuum and mop while I do the rest, but time after time he puts his chore off, his one chore out of all the things it takes to keep the house going, and I get mad. I feel like I never want to ask him to do anything for me, for fear he will put it off and hurt me with my madness. I hate being mad; it is like love goes out the door and hangs about wondering if it can ever be allowed in again. Of course it can, and sometimes within a short time, but while it is out there, it seems to be gone for good. I'm going to stop writing now. Maybe I'll go out and sit in my garden and look at things, and let love enter again somehow.

***

I am trying to find a way to write down a thought I had yesterday. Phil asked me if I was loved enough, and I said yes. I thought of the secret world inside me where I am loved incredibly by someone who seems to be real, who can even be pictured as a man, but is not known and not daydreamed about, who is just there loving me. And I thought about the music from the Theme from "Nicholas and Alexandra" which I heard once on the radio, and imagined it was the music from my secret world, where tall brown houses stood close together on cobbled winding streets in a place where the world itself seemed made of love.

There seems to be a huge secret place somewhere inside me and only certain things that I do and think in this real world also belong in that one, such as being loved by Phil or other sorts of things like observing birds or the dogs or going to Galena Creek and watching the water rushing, or seeing how the snow clings to the bare tree branches outside my window or any little secret thing I notice like the children at school, or a spider crossing the floor. Yesterday when I felt at the back of my mind a huge space full of spirit and nature, a home for me in my world, I thought that maybe that space is in everyone, and from that space come various conceptions of religion.

People used to say we use only a certain percentage of our brain's potential - well, maybe all the secret spiritual, superstitious, or religious beliefs we have are inklings from that larger space. If we had the perfect use of the unused part of our brain, we would understand all our questions, fears and all the wonder of our perceptions of the beautiful world and the sadnesses, too, of what we do that is wrong and horrible. Why do we have all that brain power that we can't use? It gives us such tantalizing inklings of perfection that we make up religions and philosophies and we see that wrong things are wrong, but why do we only get that far?

***

As I sat out in the lounge in the yard, resting from painting in my workshop I told Phil, "Even though I'm ugly, I have to keep doing something." He said, "What do you mean?" And I explained that I had looked at myself in the mirror today and seen how puffy and flabby and ugly I am, yet I still had to find things to do as if I mattered and as if people would care. Phil said he felt the same way when he sees himself; he has to overcome a feeling of being non-descript in order to keep going.

It's kind of sad. I do best when I don't glance in the mirror. Then I am just the person I am inside, not the outer covering, which looks to me like a person who doesn't count. Not that I feel other plain people don't count when I see them, but only when I see myself do I feel a certain nothingness shows in my appearance. Luckily for me and for other plain and fat people, there are many of us, all feeling nearly the same thing and so understanding each other and able to care about one another.

***

When I sat for a moment on the couch and listened to the radio, I heard an instrumental by Kenny G, who played the saxophone in a soft but jazzy way. As I listened, I felt a pulling in my chest, about life, the mystery of it, time, time passing, lives of loved ones and myself going on in their tragic courses, and why, and why does it go on in such a way, with the past stretching out behind each living and non-living thing, and the future ahead. The music explained it all without words, and I understood as long as the music went on, but as soon as it ended and a shallow tune followed, I lost the meaning of life and death that the combination of instruments, especially the saxophone with its clear notes that drift like a river and its minor notes that sound sad and complaining, had given me for about three minutes.

***

My good cat friend, Monty died. I've known Monty longer than I've known Phil, having been given the little scrawny kitten by a passenger on the Dial-A-Ride bus I drove around Hemet before I moved to Reno. It is sad to see animals I've loved and let live with me so long go - why do they have such short lives, I wonder, but because of that other animals come into my life.

Phil told me, "I want to get you a kitten. It'll be a gift from me." We searched the humane society and other adoption places, but for some reason no kittens were available. When we called about the kittens in the ads, they were already gone. Then today we visited an out of the way pet store, and there in a cage were five or six fluffy kittens of different colors. Which to choose? I took so long, Phil went out to the car to wait. I only had color on which to base my decision, until one of the little guys came up to the wire and meowed right at me. That is our new family member!

He nearly tore up the small cardboard box we carried him home in, so terribly fierce was he! "Name him William," Phil told me. That's Phil's middle name. What a delight this first day as William the kitten skipped across the bed, and whoops, dropped right over the side without knowing it. Kittens are the sweetest laughingest creatures on earth!

1997

Some weeks ago Phil told me he wasn't going to have sex anymore. He said it so coldly one afternoon, I couldn't understand him. "You mean we won't get together right now," I asked.

"I'm just not going to do it anymore. You will have to accept it."

I don't remember what brought this on. It wasn't some

meanness or anger at me; I believe his inner judgment from the dark side pestered him enough that he gave in to it - that sex was for making babies, and since we could no longer even think of having a baby, then we were done with it. In his mind, he doesn't understand the great meaning of sex as a bonding loving joyful way to stay in love together. Meanwhile, I guess he thinks that in my mind, I don't understand that we don't need the act of sex to show our love for each other.

His decision hurts me, and we've had a weekly spat about it, week after week. We have some fun interchange, a hug, a kiss maybe in bed, an "I love you" or a "You are my best one," and that leads to my pleading to go on. "Please touch me," I say.

"No, we aren't doing that anymore," he says over and over.

I begin to cry, and he tries to comfort, I struggle away and stormily hate him for sometimes more than an hour. Then my mind just gives in, my energy dissipates, and I just can't care enough to press the matter more, until next time. And in between times my heart loves him, my cheeriness blossoms again, and why not be friends, my mind seems to tell me.

I'm older now, and he's older, too, by 11 years, and he has all that medicine that might affect him, and so on and so on. But I also think to myself: what about all the old guys you hear about who have sex into their 80s? Phil is only in his 50s. Whatever the reason so it happens, and it causes a tiny break in my heart that hurts a lot and makes me mad, too. Sometimes I talk about the subject with him, sometimes he is sorry, but only a few times did he give in (twice so far).

The ability to feel joy when times are good gives me my power over the sadness that haunts my poor old far away soul. So many tears I have shed over the course of my life.

***

Debbie Bumstead

Hurray, vacation time - Tuesday Phil and I drove up to Truckee with our camping stuff. We checked in at the campgrounds at a small ticket cabin at the entrance. A girl in a green uniform, all pleasant and chirpy, explained our campsite location, and I wished I could have stayed with the Forestry Service when I had the chance when I was young and been a ranger. I have that wish often, but of course I can't go back and do what I should have done. It's hard to do what you should do.

We drove around the lane past other people camping in tents and RVs under the pines. Our site was beside some unsavory looking people all sitting at their table and staring at us as we fumbled with our tent. The tent's always hard to put up because we forget from one time to the next how it's done. After that ordeal, which we laughed about, we went into town to shop for food, and that was an ordeal in a way too, because whenever we shop together we get a little cross with each other -- I am so thrifty and Phil is so spend-thrifty. Phil said we're supposed to be having fun, and I agreed and said a fun time would be had by all and gave in.

We came back to our home under the trees and made sandwiches and sat around staring at our neighbors. It seems to be the only interesting thing to do; you are in such close proximity to these strangers all around you that you're curious, as if you were watching TV. The unsavory people consisted of a scraggly-faced man in glasses and a woman with dark curly hair, and some teenagers, who looked awful, like dope addicts. Two played ball in the lane, one a guy who hid under a bush when the Forestry Service truck went by and a girl who held her arm in a floppy way as if she'd had a stroke. This group also had a little boy about six who was blind, and the scraggly-faced guy lifted him to the table, and I watched the boy search out things to touch and play with, some cups, a ball, and then his hand searched up to a coffee pot on a burner that was apparently cold. He took the coffee

126

pot top off and was feeling it, when the man jumped up, shouted no, and swatted the boy's hands. The boy recoiled, put his arms around his dark head and soothed himself. Later there was another loud no, and I thought his little searching hands were so eager to get at things that he was causing the grown-ups to be impatient. Other times I saw the adults touching and hugging him, so I think he was OK.

There was also a little girl slightly older than the blind boy, and she had straight blond hair and wore glasses, looking like I did at ten, and she was told to walk the boy around the lane. She started off at a quick pace, but mother called for her to slow down. The little boy hopped along in a cheerful way, but his sister considered the walk a chore that she had to get done in a hurry. They went around twice, and then the girl got her bike and helmet and went riding with the two girls and two boys who were at the campsite across from us.

That campsite had a grandma taking care of about five children. One was a baby about two named Justin, who smiled at me as I walked to the restroom. The older kids made a lot of noise, which echoed cheerily in the trees along with the squawking of the jays and the chattering of the chipmunks. One time Phil said what did that kid yell, and I said I don't know what did it sound like, and Phil said it sounded like "You lying bastard," and we laughed.

I also noticed the group beyond us a ways, four young women and a mature man, a man and wife and three daughters, I thought. They all went off with knapsacks on their back, and came back later, all sturdy and doing the camping thing.

About one Phil and I changed into our shorts in our tent and drove down to the lake to swim. We blew up our air mattresses and splashed into the cold water that was nice once I got used to it. I paddled around in the gentle waves, while Phil used his mattress more like water wings and swam out further than I. A rubber boat floated by with a dad with a

Southern accent, a woman who was afraid and a little child. Someone went by in an inner tube. The trees at the edge of the cove circled round and the sky was blue.

Back at the tent we changed again. I sat in the hammock and swung, reading *Harriet the Spy*, a children's book I liked a long time ago. Phil just sat and smoked and drank up all the Snapple. We walked down to the creek and found an emerald pool. Right near there was the site of one of the cabins of the Donner Party. That history happened one winter more than a hundred years ago, deep snow, starving people, desperation, cannibalism. And now in the present in summer we saw only the pretty green water, green growing bushes, delicate little purple flowers, paths, a girl wading, trees bending over the water, rocks shining in the bottom of the creek.

We set up our new grill and cooked potatoes, corn in a can, and a steak for Phil, with toasted marshmallows afterwards. We sat around some more watching the neighbors, the chipmunks, the trees. Phil wanted coffee, so we drove out to the restaurant nearby and he had coffee while I had a sundae.

Then came the night and it was awful. My air mattress leaked, so I was soon on the hard ground. I used the portapotty and it fell under my weight. My shoulders ached, my hips, everything ached though I'd taken my medicine. I spent the night dozing a little and thinking a lot, trying to say it was OK to not sleep. When Phil woke up and had to hike to the restroom, I went with him. That was the moment most memorable -- our jolly snuggly walk to the restroom in the night, pretending to be afraid of bears or cougars, together under the pine-struck sky. While all the others slept, we were two together.

I thought it was probably about midnight and I had six more hours of this torture to go through, but when I shone the flashlight on Phil's watch it was four, only two more hours! Phil let me sleep on his mattress then, but I still didn't sleep much and was glad when I could get up. I sat in the car and read and watched the neighbors get their fires going. The grandma brought out Justin and set him in a chair all bundled in blankets and with his hood up. The man with the four young women went off with two of them carrying fishing gear. I ate graham crackers and milk.

When Phil got up, I said I couldn't have another night like that, so we packed up and didn't stay like we'd planned for another night. It was cloudy. We drove down out of the mountains and home again. I rested a lot all Wednesday, daydreaming a dream about camping with a child. His name was Glen Dillon, and he had Phil's dark eyes and red hair. I imagined him playing and riding bikes with the children who had been there at Donner Lake Campground. I imagined him swimming with us; he'd be a good swimmer even at six because I would have started him early to learn since I enjoyed swimming so much as a child. I went on and on with my daydream, how nice a boy he'd be with the Bumstead quietness, how back here at home he'd visit Daddy and call him Grandpa, how he'd play on Joe's computer, how he'd be at a Winans get-together with his cousins, and so on. How nice it'd have been for Phil and me to have had a child.

***

Phil left yesterday on his latest escape attempt, this time to Sacramento again. At first I like the days he is gone. I no longer have to listen to him tell me about his impossible business ideas (which are good except that they all require money to start that we will never in our wildest dreams have) or his impossible moving and living somewhere else and bringing me to him ideas (which also require money we don't have and never will). I also like to putter around the house without Phil around, but in the evenings and after a few days I miss him. He's a gentle presence most of the time, someone I can talk to and touch and go places with, someone who's always there to comfort me, someone to love and care about. For him I think it is the same. For awhile he likes to be rid of me, the way I get cross at him or nag him to change his habits or to do things, the annoying way I am sometimes not what he wants. Then he gets lonely for me, remembering that most of the time I'm gentle and helpful -- oh, well, so on and so on. He always comes home.

***

Today, after we shopped, Phil and I had pie at Marie's. Now the restaurant is way south by the Mall, so we hardly go anymore. When Marie Calendar's was in town, it was our place. We went there on our very first date, way back in 1982. Our first date - I can still feel the awkwardness of wondering what to say, still hear the rustle of my long hair on my corduroy jacket, still see the way Phil bent over the table to look up into my downcast eyes.

***

Sometimes I dream about our life in Gridley in 1988, Phil going to work at the furniture store each morning and me being alone to shop or write or keep house, then me going to the store at lunchtime to help for a couple of hours, then me going home, and then Phil coming home at six. Our house was neat and small, and we had the yard and the dog and the cats. And in the evenings we drove to Thrifty's for ice cream cones.

Those days are all gone.

❧Part Three ❧

Debbie Bumstead

❧Al-deb-aran House ❧
2001

They say the whole body changes every seven years, and when I look back on my life, I see it in seven year changeovers. Up to age of 7, I was growing in Hemet in the circle of the family, both good and bad, including the mess with Uncle Hersey, but then our immediate family had a beautiful year in Washington state, followed by an adventurous few years in Hemet again. When I was 14, after suffering from the break-up of my parents, I experienced a great year at school, where I was praised by teachers as a writer. Then at 21 or thereabouts came the break-up with my boyfriend, as well as graduating college, facing life, and having a nervous breakdown! At 27 came the end of loneliness with a move to Reno, meeting Phil and finding love.

About 35 or thereabouts, along came the change of my body into a broken achy sickly one, about seven years later we got a new home, and Phil's illness became the deep change in my life, and I was 54 when Phil passed away. I figure I am due for a seven year change now, as I lay to rest my man in my mind in these words I write. I am saying good-bye to my Phil, and letting him lie in his wild windblown grave with the nightly singing of coyotes nearby, while I go on as best I can in our twenty-tree home on Aldebaran Street. It is time to say good-bye, as the song goes, one of the last songs we loved together.

Aldebaran is pronounced Al - Deb - Aran not Alde-baran; this I learned early from my brother Joe who told me it was the name of a star and is mentioned in the movie *Star Wars*. Most people, even those on this street, I think, pronounce the name wrong, but my house I call Al-deb-aran House and the way I say it makes it seem like I live on a star.

In the year 2001 the 50 year old Wagon Wheel Motel sold to the University of Nevada, Reno to become a parking lot. The buildings came down very quickly, but they left the lovely redwood evergreens my brothers had planted around the perimeter of the three acres. I like to drive by and see those trees, which we used to call in fun our giant redwoods when they were just sprigs. Now they are about 25 feet tall, dark brushy forest green and healthy from good care, the only living things left except us. How strange to have experienced the incredible history, all the details, all the funny stories Grandmother told of the renters, all the joys and tribulations of my family members and my husband and me, and then to see how such an important past lies buried in the dust under the black pavement without any thought except ours as we live, gone when we die? All over the world such is happening, people die, are forgotten, buildings torn down and the present overcoming the past - how can it be tolerated, to lose so many important thoughts and life histories of men, women, and children? And yet how can it go on, but that way? It all hurts me.

But the Motel was sold, and two houses in the north valleys of Reno were purchased, one for my brothers Joe and Tim, another for Phil and me with a mother-in-law studio for Mama to live in. Tim didn't stay long with Joe in their house; he had to move into a nursing home where he spent the rest of his life. He had Huntington's Disease, a disease of the brain, inherited from a parent (our dad), and so Joe and I also feared we would end up like Tim. But we two were lucky; when a test came out, we both tested free of the gene.

When Phil and I moved into our new house then, in 2001, we were alone for a few months, while my mom stayed at the motel to supervise moving her treasures. I loved those weeks when Phil and I could yell at each other from room to room. "Phil! Where are you?" or "Debbie, come here." We were two cozy pals setting up house. We could be as noisy as we wanted, and I was free to get mad and cry noisily, too. When my mom joined us, though she was independent in her little studio at the end of the house, I became quiet and inhibited again, though Phil seemed not to mind my mama's presence at all. She herself worried about making us uncomfortable, which also made me worry about her.

Well, it was not ideal to be living with Mama, but she was quite old by then and not driving anymore, so she needed some care. Besides, she had bought the house! Really, she was also a built-in friend, and kept me company when Phil went on trips. And, when he was home, oh, how I loved gentle Phil for loving my gentle mom!

Aldebaran House is the finest house I have ever lived in, though it is just a simple ranch home of 1450 square feet, 3 bedrooms and 2 baths with a big living area. Everything about it is crisp and clean-lined. The living room ceiling slants up to a low angle peak with two big windows on one wall, a large area in the middle with furniture we brought from our furniture store days, a dark forest green leather sofa and chair, two recliners, and another big chair with an ottoman, and then tables and lamps and things. On one side wall stands the ornately carved pump organ, more than a hundred years old, that my Grandbee Bumstead gave me. On the other side wall I have my four tall wood bookcases full of a vintage children's book collection, among other books I've loved through the ages.

Debbie Bumstead

The living area is open to the dining and the kitchen, and there's a plate glass door to the patio. The patio roof is made of slats over wood beams and throws fine squares of shadow and sunshine below on the red bricks and fallen leaves from the cottonwood trees. Phil liked the house, too, liked the flat half acre yard full of trees, the pigeon coop, the P & D Coop, we called it, and the patio where Phil smoked, and inside, his sitting spot on the sofa, the kitchen with his milk and coffee easily accessed, and his study with desk and extra bed in the smallest bedroom. But he thought of the house as mine, or my mom's, and he still daydreamed about the Tudor mansion or the huge log cabin he would build for me, for my mom, when his business succeeded, whichever business or invention was topmost in his mind at the time.

There seemed no defense against Phil's schizoaffective illness cropping up and wrecking things for him, even as we felt contented in our home on Aldebaran Drive. If I could, I would have stripped all that dark ill part from his brain, and he would have been free to be what he truly was. Maybe we all have that trouble wrapped up in our minds in one shape or another, but I was looking at Phil and watching torture curling around the edges of a good life, and I wished I could help. It's funny, but I had a daydream in which I was a tiny being inside Phil, directing him, and keeping him from suffering and consequently keeping him home with me. But that was only a daydream.

136

My Huckleberry Friend ⚡
2002 Memories

In June of 2002, Phil's mom, Doris, died of cancer. When Phil's sister called from Fallon to tell us, Phil began to cry. We both cried - and then we began to talk about the fun trip to Washington state we'd made with her the year before, all the many times we took her to Donner Lake for picnics, her overnight stays with us, going out to eat, watching VCR movies. All these things we'd done with her since Phil's dad had died some ten years ago, and she had become a person on her own.

I remembered the first time I met her and Dad, her nervousness. I thought of the Gridley Days of the furniture store, when I observed and sometimes got secretly mad at them both, he for being a grumpy old gus, and she for submitting to his every whim. After he died, the first change I noticed was she began to read books. I asked about it, and she told me she'd always loved to read, but Dad didn't really like her to. Ooo, I felt angry - why should a guy complain about something so innocently pleasurable as reading? And, also, why didn't she stand up to him about it? But these were thoughts I kept to myself.

After Dad died, Doris became a very close friend to me, so that now, as I cried about her death, I told Phil, "I won't ever see her bright berry eyes again, or have someone to talk to about you."

Phil sobbed. "She's gone," he said.

***

No one looking at Phil, or listening to him or knowing his past would have called him a Mama's Boy type of man. He wasn't a Mama's Boy in that sense, but I do believe she was the most important person in his life, and had been, of course, when he was a child, but also many times since when his illness hurt him. He often told me I was his only friend, but I did feel a little jealous of his concern for his mom. For instance, at Christmas he worried over getting her a meaningful and expensive present, while for me, he gave me a little money and said buy what you want. Any other minor comparison like that would hurt my feelings. But I tried to get over my jealousy, or at least to understand it, because I loved her, too.

Only a month after Doris's death, Phil got on a bus to Alaska - yes, Alaska! Oh, how far he wanted to get away from his sorrow and failure! Before leaving, he named my new kitten, a tiny Himalayan ball of fur, Chamois, and I was distracted by Chamois's shenanigans with William, Tugger, and Bridget somewhat but not enough as Phil traveled north alone and far. I dreamed one night that I was a sparrow, able to fly after Phil, following him away. I woke from this dream crying in the middle of the night.

But after several days of travel, Phil was back. I should have learned by now, I told myself, to just trust that he'd be home soon. Indeed he should have learned by then, too, that nowhere was as good as home, where the heart waited to love him again. But we both struggled on, never learning from our mistakes, I don't know why.

"It's summertime and we haven't gone to Donner Lake yet," I said to Phil after a week or so. So, we drove up to

Truckee, all without Doris this time. We stopped at the Safeway and bought deli salads - potato for me and seafood for him, cookies - animal for him, oreo bars for me, milk, cake, a jug of water, and a little bag of fritos. We drove to the lodge we had stayed in once before, that looked like a Swiss Chalet, and paid for a room. I put my swimsuit on under my clothes before we headed up the block to the lake. We set up our chairs at our favorite spot, the same table we had had when Doris came with us last year.

"Oh, Phil," I said, almost crying, "remember how excited she was to go in swimming with us? How afterwards she loved to tell the rest of the family that she'd been swimming at her great age?"

"Mom was a sport," Phil said, fondly.

We ate our goodies and watched children splashing, heard their calling laughing voices. I saw two thin slips of girls about five and a boy of two crossing the parking lot to join the crowd; how sweet and fragile they look from a distance, I thought, but it's only when you're responsible for them that they become work.

Phil and I, too, moved our chairs up by the beach after we took turns blowing up the air mattress. I wished Phil would join me in the water, but he wouldn't, so it took some time for me to get the courage to dive in. I remembered last year, how Doris and I with our pink blow-up rafts and Phil in shorts and t-shirt swam together. Now I went out on my own, but I found I liked drifting, rising with the waves, riding the swells up and down. The water was so shallow, I could put my feet down to steady myself. I let my focus free and gazed around at the surrounding trees that dark green I loved with the flickering water below, and the calls of children and birds softened into a cosmic music that might have relaxed me, but I was still thinking of Doris and tears slipped down the sides of my face. I remembered the two or three times she had said I was an angel. I would laugh, as if she were teasing me, and she'd say,

"But you are an angel. You are an angel come to help Philip."

After my swim, Phil and I each took a camera, and we had a contest for best photo. I took pictures of the scenery. Phil mostly snapped photos of me, including several showing my cleavage as I sat at the picnic table in my swimsuit. I took a photo of Phil that turned out the best of all, I thought; he stands against the background of green in his denim shirt, tall, straight, but older, 60 this year, his smile crookedly shy and his face, his expression calm. I wonder now how such a pleasant calm image could hide the inner war of his mind. Maybe that day, that moment, he was himself.

Soon after our contest, I suddenly had to lie down; I ached badly, my legs, my back, and nothing would help but a rest. We went back to the Chalet room where I watched TV and Phil sat on the porch smoking. In the evening at bedtime, we got into bed, and I felt better. I wished with all my heart we could cuddle sexually, make love, but to keep peace I didn't even ask. It passes my mind, now, that I was as weak as Doris had been with Phil's Dad. I could not stand up for myself, not against my man's stubborn selfishness. But perhaps like Doris, I didn't want to believe it was selfishness and grumpy old man-ish-ness; it was maybe my fault for wanting something he did not like. Could that be true?

But how did I get onto that subject? I meant this to be about our grief for Doris. However, I might add this memory, of me arguing for sex by saying, "Your mom and dad probably still made love at our age." And Phil replying, "Probably," but remaining unconvinced. And another memory pops up, the time I told him, "I probably gained all this weight because you stopped making love to me," and again he said, "Probably," and added, "I'm sorry, but I still love you."

Phil wasn't through with trying to get the farthest he could from himself, either; he soon took a trip to Maine, across the whole country to try out a school. Looking back, I see how he was caught in a loop of feeling as if he were in his 20s, the time when a fellow seeks out his way forward; he tried one school or another, or one business idea or another, believing that he was on his way at last. At 60 years old maybe his healthy self knew he should retire from this frantic quest, but the illness drove him on. He spent two weeks going to Maine and coming back, and when he got back, he told me he'd like to try Maine again in a little while! My poor man!

I don't remember if he tried Maine again, but he traveled often, so much so that in my journal entry of March 25, 2003, I was writing, "Phil has been on a couple more trips, but as we tried to figure out when and where tonight, neither of us can remember. Now he's staying with ideas about starting a little business called Grocery-Go-Getters." As I recall Grocery-Go-Getters was one of the inventions/businesses that got an asterisk in his funeral book - meaning I saw it created later on by someone else. Meanwhile, I also started a business of painting pictures of different dog breeds in humorous or colorful renditions that sold well online.

So, I painted and Phil dreamed and traveled and came home again for awhile. When he was home, life was bliss for me, mostly. We spoke of Doris often, and I remember in particular driving one day with Phil from our north valley home down into Reno when the radio began to play *Moon River*. The music, the lyrics, swooned into me with sadness; "My huckleberry friend," what a beautiful phrase, describing perfectly my friendship with Phil's mom - how she loved to go on adventures with us, how she was game for anything, and how she put me at ease by just being a plain and lovely person. I began to sob, as I hadn't since her death, and let my grief consume me for a comforting moment. Then I could let her go on. My huckleberry friend.

I don't know if his mom's death started Phil's descent, that maybe he was not able to find peace about it. Maybe it was his age, or a change of medicine, or something that went boing in his brain, but from my view back to 2002 and up to 2008 when he passed away, I feel Doris's absence left a hole inside Phil, and he slowly dropped down, down into it, in both mind and body. I couldn't stop the descent, though I tried mightily.

⋊Adventures of the Night ⋉
Dreams from 2003 Journal

Phil's warm hands massaged my back, down down around and in between, we came together just like in the past, just as if he hadn't decided to stop making love, all the warm sexual feelings of love so real and sweet. It was just a dream.

Then I dreamed that Phil and I were at the beach. Various fish flopped out of the water and Phil picked them up by the tails and tossed them into an aquarium. But one fish I didn't want. This fish then turned into a sea urchin skeleton yet it was alive and trying to get back at me. I kicked it viciously off our porch, thinking I'd get rid of it. Then Phil and I and our two children were in the house when the urchin broke in. It was gigantic, breaking down the walls, crushing us. I felt myself suffocating.

**

We are watching Camelot and when Guinevere went into her locked garden, I remembered a nice dream last night of a corner garden with a brick wall around it and a wooden door for a gate. The garden was small but pleasant with trees and flowers.

**

Debbie Bumstead

I dreamed something about hiking in the Hemet hills last night. A few nights ago I dreamed I was walking under rainy dripping trees. It was pretty. The dream got dangerous, though, when a wall of water rushed toward me. I saw some people get swept up. I ran onto a woman's porch and she and I stood there watching the water rush by.

**

This morning about 3:30 Phil got in a taxi for the Greyhound station. He's on his way across the country on a pipedream. I had three night dreams before he left that he had changed his mind, and another afterward that he'd come back. I know he will be back soon, but it's hard anyway.

I slept so lightly I remembered some more dreams, which shows me I must dream a lot of stories each night that I never remember usually. In one I was a younger woman going up to a wealthy man's apartment. I looked around at his living room - art everywhere. Then we went in his bedroom for him to get something out of a huge closet, and I saw he had two great big four poster beds set near each other. Both were unmade. The man said one was for lovin' and the other was for sleepin'.

I dreamed I was cozily curled up in my own bed, all wrapped in fuzzy white, feeling like a bunny, and a voice kept calling in a whispery voice, "Mrs. Winans, Mrs. Winans."

I dreamed I was a young slim woman dressed in a navy blue dress going to work at a company. I was searching up and down halls for my office - the building was designed with a hub in the middle and hallways going like spokes from the hub. Finally I got back to the President's area, and he and the other workers laughed and said, "Happy Birthday!" They gave me a bag of cookies. There my office in a glass room. I was the person who made the company newspaper.

Finally I dreamed I was in my bedroom and a friend from a long time ago, Annette, was there, too. We were close and

144

knew all about each other. It felt good to have such a close girlfriend. Then we looked out the window. I said, "There's a landslide." I saw mud coming down a hillside at us, but didn't feel afraid. Then three propane tanks fell down and I held my breath but they went over into a canyon. People were trying to contain them, but then there were explosions all up and down the green canyon. Then I woke up for good.

**

Early this morning I had a wonderful dream, though it seems tame to me now. At first I was walking up to our old house in Hemet but all around it a cathedral of trees rose way up in the sky, and mists and stained-glass colors filled the air. Then I entered a community hall where a celebration was going on. My young son came to me and asked me to dance. I saw my high school English teacher Miss Kerr watching me and I was proud of Phil's and my little boy. I told the boy I was tired and I went to sit on a stool by the tables. Then our blonde-haired daughter came up to me and climbed into my lap. She was about 10 and the boy about 8. The beauty of the dream was the natural joy of feeling I had children.

Phil's sister and her husband were there. Her husband sang in a quartet. They sang "Pick a little peck a little" from *The Music Man*, which was funny, as it is a gossipy ladies' song.

Finally as the graduation of the children began, Phil came in. Our son called out "Dad!" so loud, everyone laughed. I woke up feeling what a good daydream sort of dream it had been.

**

Two spy dreams. In one a man escaped from some people who were experimenting with secret formulas. He, with me following along, tried to repeat his tracks to find out what the bad guys were up to. There was a busy street of shoppers, mysterious little shops, us ducking in and out of places, a bookstore with a suspicious bookseller, and other exciting details.

In the second dream, I was a spy. It was night, dark sky, dark green grass, buildings that were like the dorm at Cal Western College, and me, young, slim, running. I ran swiftly along the grass between the buildings downhill. Oh, I felt so wonderful, running so quickly in the beautiful night, unafraid, my legs striding forward strongly. It seemed as if my unconscious mind realized I loved the sensation of running, so it made the running of the dream last and last. I came down to a street in a neighborhood of small houses. Then I woke up.

**

Dream: another in a series of bad dreams about Random Acres in the hills of Hemet. Uncle Hersey was a Nazi along with some other Nazi guys up at the place where we camped once. I was in danger and ran down the old path toward Grandbee and Grandpa's house. But they were too close to getting us. I told the child with me to find a hiding place in the rocks, curl up, and freeze. I did the same. I curled up under a sagebrush. All I could see was gravel and things on the ground. I fell asleep. I woke up in the dark and heard a boot stepping next to me. I knew I had to make a break for it, so the child and I ran down the path (I can still remember every curve, every boulder of that path). I knew we couldn't stop at the house because a Nazi guy was living there. He looked like Claude Rains (I just saw *Notorious* on TV.) Somehow we escaped up the dirt road. There was more to the dream, all the details, so amazing, just like real life.

I loved Random Acres, but nearly every dream I have about the hilly rocky old Hemet country is very bad.

**

Last night I dreamed I was at the ocean near my friend Debbie's place above San Diego. First I saw a film of some people swimming naked with their clothes floating around them. It looked very relaxing. Then it seemed this old guru type guy started a group where you'd go swim in warm water with your clothes off but in the water, too.

I met the group in a room that had French doors that led to a patio above the ocean. I really liked the room. The man led us all down a hallway and as we went we undressed. Of course I was slim and young, so didn't mind getting naked. But the pool we were to swim in looked stagnant with weeds and bugs floating on top. The pond was like a circular moat. Everybody dived in.

Now in my dream I swam fast around and around, my arms going like windmills. I felt good. I raced people and won, I splashed people and stole things. I was having so much fun in the water.

**

Last night I started reading a book set in the 1700s, a sequel to *Pride and Prejudice* about girls trying to get men, titled *Mr. Darcy's Daughters*.

Then during the night I had a wild and fun dream. A handsome man with long dark hair, who wore 18th century clothes with tall black boots was seeing to an overturned carriage. Then he went into his house and ran through rooms, one sumptuous room leading into another, and the doors opened for him, and if they didn't he kicked them open with his boot. The suspense of the dream built with every room until he threw open the door of his study where I stood waiting, dressed in my finery, and he took me in his arms. He kissed me hard, and I could feel his arousal against my body. I was aroused, too, and then I woke up.

❧Tortures of the Mind ❧
2004 & 2005 Memories

In the spring of 2003 after several journeys, Phil was home, but his "heart hurt." I asked what it meant when he said his heart hurt, and he told me he was depressed. I sat down with him, close against his side on the sofa, and he hugged me to him, rubbed his hand up and down my arm. What could I do for him? The days slipped by, and we lived by doing one thing and then another at our Aldebaran House.

Then, it was late December 3, 2003, after a fun day shopping and fixing the Christmas tree, that Phil sat down and got very quiet for a couple hours. At bed-time he said he didn't feel well, and he was going to the hospital to check into the mental health ward. In my journal entry, I see that with the doctor's approval, Phil had been trying to cut down on his medicines. So this was the reason for this particular visit - the reduction of his mental health meds wasn't working. He came home the next day, encouraged by his doctors with new medicine.

But even new medicines didn't help Phil. In February of 2004 he stayed at the hospital for about three weeks. He felt like he wanted to take his life - to be done with the voices that spoke to him inside his mind. What was that like, I wonder? To hear someone talking inside to you, someone who seems as real as someone outside your body, or maybe even more real, because now those outside fade away with the force of the inner ones. And from Phil's description, the people inside were not kind; they were cruel and angry, sad and accusing. Hallucinations also plagued him, as I learned when his psychologist called and told me Phil spoke of a third eye in the middle of his forehead that some villain was trying to dig out. Poor, poor Phil, it made my heart hurt to think of his suffering. He phoned me each day, though, and we had simple homely conversations.

The hospital had a courtyard in the middle of the building, and Phil would go sit there afternoons and feed the wild pigeons that came for treats. He talked about them over the phone, and we began to plan to have Birmingham Rollers here at home again, as we had had on the motel property ten years ago.

On the Internet I found a man in Washington who sold us the birds, which came in the overnight mail. Phil looked forward to caring for them, watching them raise young, flying them. My brother Joe built us a big aviary in the back yard, and when Phil came home, feeling better, though still suffering, each day he and I wandered back to the P & D Coop and watched the four pigeons: blue bars, TopsyTurvy and feisty hen, RoundAbout, and red bars, RolyPoly, and his mate UpsyDaisy. We named them for Phil's wild horse bunch stories.

As the pigeons mated and began to sit on eggs in their homemade nest boxes, Phil lost hope again. In early May I took him to the hospital after he told me, "I want to kill myself but my love for you keeps me from going through with it." All I could do was hug him and make sure he saw the doctors again. The next day over the phone he said he felt better, which made my own spirits rise. Still I began to cry when he added, "The intake doctor said I might have to go to a home for awhile, because I keep coming here."

"Oh, My Redwood Heart!"

When he was discharged, he still didn't feel well. Despite my begging him not to go, he took his May disability check and got on the bus to travel east. I wish I'd written down his reasoning for the trip. But away he went, and he stayed away a long time because he checked into a VA Domiciliary in Knoxville, Iowa and they kept him. I believe he had once visited this Dom before briefly on another trip; perhaps he had felt safe there and figured this was the "home" he needed to be in.

I was so lonely for him I tried the patient 800 number to talk to him every day. That patient phone was always busy, it seemed! Then I got him one morning and cried almost the whole time we talked. I begged him to come home, but he said he couldn't, he felt too much pain in Nevada. He said he was being entered into a six week program in which he would have classes and groups and crafts. I cried quietly, asking myself was I to be alone again without my secret sharer? I wanted Phil to get help, but I was so darn sorry for myself. After more tears on both sides and telling each other we loved one another, we hung up.

My days went on; I painted and sold pictures online; I kept up with house, family, and friends; and I ached, from an injured knee as well as the fibromyalgia. They were lonely old days, but I went along with them. A baby pigeon hatched and survived - TipTop I named it, and I held it on my lap each time I went down to the Coop. The little creature would strain his neck this way and that to see all the world around him, and laughter at its cuteness bubbled in my throat. How I wished Phil were there to see, to share.

Another day, another call: I could feel him right against my ear, his easy voice seeming to be close to me, yet he was miles and miles away in the white hallway of a mental asylum. "I wish you would come home," I told him.

"I feel too much pain," Phil said His words were wise, I knew, but impossible, too. "I left for your sake as a desperate act," he told me. "If I'd stayed, I would have committed suicide and you would have had to grieve. Now with me away, at least you can know that I am alive."

"Yes, but -"

"I hate to be apart, too," Phil said, more forcefully. "I hate to do this to you, but it is necessary."

I felt calmer as he spoke. "When you put it that way," I told him, "I understand. But I wish it could better."

Phil changed the subject. He said, "I'm going to work four hours a day at the hospital laundry. I'll be making a little money."

May led into June, then July. We talked two or three times a week. I still cried a lot, unable to accept his absence.

"You should get a little mad at me," Phil said on one call, "so you won't miss me so much."

**

By September Phil had moved into a halfway program that let him have his own apartment in the little town of Knoxville. But he wasn't doing as well as he professed. One day he called to ask me to send him 300.00 for a bus ticket home. He seemed to have changed his mind about never coming back.

He told me, "I'm just not making it here, and I want to be with you again." I felt so happy at his words that a burden of loneliness lifted from my shoulders.

But - three days later I was living a nightmare. Phil had not been on the bus; he was not at the station in downtown Reno when I went to pick him up. I drove back home and waited - but no call came. Finally I called his helper in Knoxville, and she checked the VA hospitals to see if he'd gone to another one. No sign there, but he had been seen at the Knoxville bus station several days ago. She told me to make a missing person report, so I did, and then waited, suffering all the next day with tears and sadness thinking the worst and trying to think the best. The best would be if he had gotten on the wrong bus or missed a connection but why wouldn't he call? The worst would be that his cheer about coming home was an act, and he was really depressed and planned to take his life.

The next day I waited again for Phil to call from the bus station. No call. I called his sister and told her he was missing. She thought for sure he was on a bus somewhere, that he got delayed somehow. So much uncertainty made my heart and stomach feel sick with dread. I cried often and felt frozen in time, like I couldn't move for fear of missing some thought that could bring him home to me.

Though I was afraid he'd killed himself, how impossible that sounded. He was so sick before, and wanted to buy a gun, but instead he went into the hospital. How he had suffered! I felt haunted by his last words to me on the phone. I kept saying how happy I was he was coming home, but he seemed sad. I said to him that he didn't sound very glad and he replied, "I'm glad." A pause and then he added: "I don't want to hurt you, Debbie. I never want to hurt you." But now, I was hurt.

Very early the next morning a kind police detective called me and said that Phil had been seen at the Canadian border. His destination was Prince George, B.C. and he was to be back in the U.S. by Sept 28. I had no idea why he'd gone up there, but I felt such a relief I could have jumped for joy. All the sorrow and tears left me at the news.

When Phil's social worker in Knoxville called later, we talked a long time. She knew Phil to a T. She told me next time to buy the ticket myself instead of sending him money. Oh, my Phil, Phil, Phil!

Then a couple of days later, my bad man called from Canada. Phil said he'd made a mistake and he was sorry. He decided to go back to Knoxville, Iowa instead of coming to Reno. I said, "It's OK. But I feel so sad." First I had been full of happiness that he was coming home, then unrelenting sorrow at his disappearance, followed by shock when the detective called, and now I only felt tired-out sadness. I knew it would be best for him to go back to the hospital, if he was going to be sick like this.

**

In October of 2004 Phil did come home for a short time. He helped me prepare for and get through my knee replacement operation, but I could tell he wasn't very well. His face held that expression of pain, a kind of wince, which meant to me he was suffering and looking inward to see if there were anything he could do for himself. While I was in the rehabilitation center wincing in my own pain, Phil visited me one more time and said he had to leave. Back to Knoxville.

I was a mess myself, though I liked my new knee. A deep anxiousness filled with sadness and really, I guess, misery overtook my mind and heart. I'd been at home hobbling around with a walker as the new year began, when I just fell into constant tearfulness. I wailed to myself when I was alone, and then even in front of my mom, and finally one day when my brother Joe was over, I just sat in my chair and cried. Joe and Mama decided I needed a doctor, but the doctor wasn't in, so we were told to go to the emergency room. So here I was, going to the hospital like Phil!

I was assigned to attend an outpatient program at an annex nearby, and there I went three mornings a week for lectures and talk in a big group where there was hardly ever time for shy me. But I got better right away with medicine and something else to do besides mope, and when I left, I started seeing a psychologist individually. I fell in love with her, or since she called that kind of love transference, I guess I fell in transference with her, and she helped me find out about myself, more than I'd ever known.

With Phil now staying long term in Iowa, I needed someone else to think about, and my psychologist also encouraged me to do other outside activities. I started going to warm pool exercise twice a week and then became a volunteer one morning a week with a first grade classroom. All I tried led to joyful moments and gave me other people to care about besides Phil. But I still cried everyday for him. We still talked on the phone often. I sent him care packages. His doctor and social workers spoke to me. Poor Phil still suffered, now with anger at not being allowed to leave on his own, now with acquiescence and gentle sadness, one day telling me never to call again, he was tired of worrying about me, and the next praising my kindness and loyalty.

This went on for nearly a year. A year.

**

A year is a long time in pigeon life. RolyPoly and his mate, and RoundAbout with hers had several babies that grew and sometimes had babies themselves, until there were about 20 pigeons in the Coop. I still enjoyed going to sit inside and watch them take baths, build nests, and fuss among themselves, but now I had a new activity for them: letting them fly free. My brother helped to make a special area for the non-breeders and we put in a window with a metal contraption that trapped the pigeons inside again as they pushed at the bars to get in to feed. I'd shoo them out in the mornings, sit in my chair and watch them fly against blue sky or cloud for awhile. Many were red, some blue, and a few were striking with white patches. SkyRoller was a pale red bar, beautiful. He, though, had too much of the gene to roll and rolled right down into the ground one day and injured himself. I retired him to the breeder's part of the coop, and he was a very funny puffed up fellow without a mate. He hogged the baths, going from one to the other to push out the other birds, who'd go back to the first bath, and he'd hurry over to take over that one again. I loved pigeon watching. The handsome gentleness of the birds along with the low purr of their cooing reminded me of Phil.

❧Across a Crowded Room ☙
2005-06 Memories

Not some enchanted evening, but one enchanted afternoon at the crowded Reno airport, I sat in the lobby area with my eyes glued to the opening from the incoming gates across the room, and I saw Phil. Hundreds of people, all moving along, from my bench to the far side, and only one pair of eyes met mine. There was Phil, looking thin, worn, gray, but so much the man I loved, our smiles blossomed in the big room like flowers in spring.

"Who can explain it? Who can tell you why?" "When you have found your true love, then fly to his side." "When you have found him, never let him go." So many lines in the song *Some Enchanted Evening* seemed to fit our romance, right from the beginning, when we had decided this was "our song." When our eyes met that moment at the airport, after Phil's year long stay in the Iowa VA Dom, both of us thought the same thought, recognizing our enchanted reunion.

It had happened because one of the social workers took time to review Phil's case, and called me to say, "Phil needs to be with his family." He set up someone to escort Phil all the way to Reno, to make sure he didn't take off for Canada or somewhere else. And my job, the social worker said, was to be strict with Phil's money and never give him enough to take a trip. Easy for him to say.

I think the actual reason he was sent home was his health. Immediately after our hug in the airport lobby and our goodbye to the man who had accompanied him here, Phil had to take a minute to get his breath. He breathed in long and hard and held his hand to his chest. "What's wrong?" I asked, and he told me he didn't know, but they wanted him to go to the VA as soon as he could. "You've lost so much weight!" I exclaimed. Phil had lost his big tummy and the round cheeks of his face; he looked handsome in a thinner, grayer way. His dark cherry eyes, though, as usual sparkled sharp at me, and I suppose he noticed my dark blue eyes looking with love back at him. There we were - both smiling to beat the band, together at last.

And there he was, at Aldebaran House, in his spot on the couch across from the chair I mostly sat in, just as he had been before. My dearest man, home. I left my chair, and we sat by each other on the couch, chatted, laughed, ate some dinner and treats; Phil fixed his coffee, and for the moment, life was bliss.

***

A few days later, Phil and I learned that he had a lung infection called an empyema, which was a bunch of pus stuck in his lung that needed to be drained in an operation. It was a simple procedure, the doctors told us, and would cure the problem.

But Phil refused to have the operation. "No," he said over and over again, as I begged him to see reason. Some more doctors had him in to explain how the operation would save him from certain death. He was going to die, if he didn't get that empyema drained, they said. "No," Phil repeated. Then Phil's sister and brother came to our house to try to talk him into going in for the cure, but Phil still said no. He said he was afraid he wouldn't survive the operation. "But you won't survive if you don't have it!" I cried. "No," was his answer.

The doctors were able to get Phil to agree to a tube in his chest, and then he was prescribed high-powered antibiotics, and sent home to die. That's how it was for me, you see. Suffer his absence for a year and now suffer his death. Suffer, girl, suffer! Maybe that's how I see it now, but at the time, some guardian nurse developed inside me to take care of Phil. I felt a kind of calm and practicality take over, and as Phil weakened more and more, a great love and compassion filled me to the top.

There he lay in the bed, mostly sleeping, sometimes gibbering a little nonsense, and then waking up to find me there for comfort. I helped him eat and drink, go to the bathroom, and come sit in the living room awhile. His sister and brother came back to visit, and that was a good day. They talked about old times, in Red Bluff, at the camp, at the Montana Ranch. Phil looked sweet, sitting by the window, his smile stretching across his thin face. When he said he better go lie down for a bit, there were hugs and tears and the family left.

The hospice people called to set up with Phil, but Phil refused their help. "They will help us," I said. "No," he replied. "I don't want all those people hanging over me waiting for me to die." "OK," I agreed. After all, it was his life, and I didn't especially want them all around, either.

The worst night found me waking up to thumping noises. Phil had gotten lost in the hallway, banging against the walls and opening up my mom's door by mistake, on his way back from the bathroom. Gently, my mom and I led him back to bed.

One early morning, as Phil and I slept, I had a dream that I was sitting on the bed near the open window. The Venetian blinds and the wispy curtains were blowing gently back and forth in a breeze. In back of me, Phil slept; I felt alone, but peaceful, accepting the reality of imminent death.

But - Phil didn't die. Phil survived the empyema, and we found life could go on after all. Phil didn't die; the antibiotics had done their good work, and bit by bit Phil improved. Someone said maybe Phil knew his body could not take an operation; maybe he knew that he could get well without it. I told Phil he could say to everyone, "I told you so," but Phil took his recovery quietly, without gloating.

***

Still, as Phil's physical health improved, his mental health remained scrambled. He began spending more days awake, working on his ideas and driving me mad with them. He wanted me to look up magazines on the Internet, so as to send an ad asking for investment in all his amazing inventions. That wasn't the kookiest part - no, he wanted the ad in English magazines, because he planned to move to England. And I didn't want to do any sort of research for him, so he got angry at me, even to the point of cussing. Oh, gosh, my poor man. Where was my gentle fellow, so wise and kind? His mind was so mixed up, he just wasn't my Phil. Days went by and I felt like a cat being rubbed the wrong way with static electricity pinging all over me.

I remembered the advice of the social worker, that I was not to give Phil enough money to go on a trip. I was Phil's payee; I was in charge and legally had the right to make decisions about how the money was to be used. OK, but it was too hard. First, Phil felt like a man, and to me he seemed to be a man; how was I to treat him as a child who needs guidance and rules? Second, his complaints and anger wore me down. When I told him no, he couldn't have his money to go to Canada again, he told me he was going to get a lawyer to take me off as payee. He threatened divorce, and told me he wanted to get his own place somewhere.

"You were so nice to me when I was sick, but now you're

all mean," he told me.

"When you were sick, you weren't talking about leaving," I replied. How was I supposed to be happy that he wanted to leave?

Then he didn't go for his labwork and got mad when I tried to get him to agree to seeing the doctors later in the week. He insisted he was not sick. Then, pacing, pacing, he talked to himself, repeating his wish to leave, have control of his money, get away from me before I made him go in the hospital. When he was like that, I hardly cared what he did. Was I supposed to bear everything?

I wasn't alone with my worries, though, since I shared with family, friends and my own psychologist each week. Each hour my therapist and I talked about the situation with Phil. We talked about what options I had - whether to let Phil go on his trip and possibly get sicker or whether to call the police to take him into the hospital, which would mean he'd be angry with me.

Then the therapist surprised me by saying, "And I'd like to say, you could kick him out."

She said it so firmly, I was incredulous and exclaimed, "What?"

"Kick him out," she repeated. "I can't see you doing it, but you would have every right. He is in the wrong here and he's been taking advantage of you for years."

I started crying at all my thoughts of how good Phil could be and had been to me, how sometimes I did feel like kicking him out, but my love for him made me care about him.

"You feel guilty that you can't care for Phil anymore," my doctor said, "but caring for someone with mental illness is different from caring for a spouse with an empyema or cancer or some illness like that. Phil's behavior, getting mad, especially, makes it different."

When I repeated this conversation to a friend of mine who was also a counselor, she agreed and said she'd known many families who simply couldn't care for their loved one with mental illness, and that I'd tried bravely and lovingly for a long time.

At home a good day would encourage me. Phil was pleasantly occupied with his thoughts, in a nice mood, and talking out loud a little but not too noisily. When we lay down for a nap, I told him how I was taking stock of my own life. "We've have had some good times together lately, like our outing for ice cream and to the bookstore or holding each other in bed," I said, snuggling against him. "My volunteering in the first grade classroom makes me feel happy, my pool exercise had led me to knowing more people. And the therapist has helped me go forward."

Phil listened kindly and talked back agreeably, but the next day he was depressed again. Nothing cheered him. While I was busy doing little things around the house, he paced back and forth and became more and more angry.

Even though I knew nowadays people used curse words easily, even nice people, Phil and I had never taken up cursing. So it was scary for me when he got mad enough to cuss. When I said no one more time to Phil's request for trip money, he blurted out, "You don't do a fucking thing. Son of a bitch. I'm going to get a lawyer and take all the money. I don't want to be married to someone who won't help me."

I froze up inside. A person can only stand so much till she becomes numb. The good things I'd just mentioned the day before fell in shreds, as I felt I truly didn't have anything to look forward to. Somehow the loss of Phil's love left me aimless. It had happened many times in the past. It always came back, his love. But this time I was worn down.

He wore at me so much from then on, that I suddenly said one day, "OK, OK, take your money and do what you want! But you can't live here anymore. You have to get a room in town when you come back, and you will come back!"

Oh, no, he was sure he'd make it this time. Though he was

still thin, sick, and weak, he took his money and made his escape.

I was only human after all; I couldn't take some things, let's face it. I was still a good person. I had tried as long as I could. I had borne as much as I could. Now he was traveling again, on the long gray bus, trying to get away. And I didn't care. I did care, but I couldn't control him. I had to let him go.

❧Project Oberon ❧
2006-2007 Memories

A week later Phil was in Reno again, calling me from the bus station. When I told him he couldn't live here anymore, he mumbled, "Where'm I going?"

"You can stay here today and tonight," I said, relenting, but I knew I was still strong, and we would have to work together to get him a new place.

In all that week he'd been gone, he hadn't taken even one of his necessary medicines. He was psychotic, I knew, the moment I picked him up at the station. He looked grimy, tall and bulky in his great green parka, hauling his luggage, his red beard bristly and curly hair uncombed, but it was his expression and speech that told me he was not conscious in his normal way. He had a silly vacant smile and every word he said was mumbly and hardly understandable. When we got home, Phil let me guide him as if a toddler into the house to sit at the table. I made him a meal, and unpacked his medicines for him to start. "Tomorrow we'll look for a room," I reminded him. He was very friendly, acquiescing to anything I said, and I felt thankful his anger had gone, at least for now.

I put the proposed boundary (as my therapist called it) off one more day, since Phil went to bed and slept for 24 hours. Then on Monday he sat at the table again, and I reminded him he would have to live somewhere else. He didn't understand and could only speak nonsense.

"You are going to have to go to the hospital," I told him.

"No," he said.

"Please, Phil," I begged. "You know you need to."

"Let me alone."

I stood next to his chair, put my arm around his shoulder and my cheek against his. All my anger and bitterness suddenly fell from my mind, too, and the compassion I'd felt when he was so sick physically rose in my heart. He was so so sick, but what was the answer for him? Darling man. To suffer and struggle through this mire of mental illness. I wished I could enter his mind with a pack of special tools to fix all the wrong turns and broken links inside him. But I couldn't, and I needed help.

Because my therapist had suggested I might call the police, I was able to consider it. When I told Phil, he said to go ahead, but he wasn't moving. The policewoman on the phone said to try an ambulance first, but in the end it was a group affair: both police and ambulance workers came to the house, all of them in uniform with various items all belted around them clanking, and they stood in a ring around Phil, hands on hips, reasoning with him to come along.

"No," he said.

"Come on, Phil!" I said in a teasing way, and I grabbed his shoulders and tried to pull him up to his feet. No movement.

Someone began to talk to him as a normal person, to which Phil began telling them all a jumbled view of religion. He was so sweet-natured about it and so friendly that everyone remained gentle for Phil, even though it looked hopeless.

One of the ambulance workers said, "If we could just get him to the door and onto the gurney, we could strap him on."

This suggestion seemed to come through to Phil's rational mind. He said, "I'm not moving. You will have to carry me."

There was an instant release of tension in all the workers. Now they saw a way that wouldn't include force and argument. Everyone gathered closer to Phil and simply lifted him in a sitting position and carried him to the gurney on the porch. Phil didn't struggle, though he went on with his philosophizing. Away they wheeled him to the ambulance.

"I'm so glad that was easy," the policeperson said to me. "Sometimes these matters escalate."

I thanked them all as they left and then followed in our car. When I got to the hospital, Phil was strapped into a bed in the ER. He held no anger towards me, so we talked simply, I about what was going on in his immediate life, and he about the bigger aspects of Life. He laughed when he tried to move his arms because they were strapped down and he couldn't scratch an itch on his forehead. I smoothed his forehead awhile with my hand, and we waited. I was given several forms to fill out, and in every one of them, I wrote a note that I couldn't take care of Phil anymore and he had to live somewhere else. I don't know if anyone noticed, but soon they sent him off to the mental health hospital he'd been in before here in Reno.

I drove home. At home I lay down and rested. Oh, my goodness, what an ordeal for both Phil and me, I thought. But I had done something strong, now I could breathe quietly again. Phil would be safe, and I would be able to take the next step in my plan when it came.

***

It was a secret plan that I hadn't even told the therapist about, created by a selfish part inside me that recognized I had been pushed to the limit. This part was working to make me free, despite the rest of me remaining kind and sacrificing. Secretly this part of me plotted and planned my own escape.

I called my plan Project Oberon after a dream I'd had about the king of fairies one night a couple of weeks before I had given in to Phil's trip. In the dream I was a fairy girl flying from San Diego up to Hemet. I swooped low, flew high, and when I got to downtown Hemet I saw other fairy folk lounging on the flat roofs of the stores. I thought, what do you know, even plain old Hemet has fairies. Some of them joined me in fun and we flew along Buena Vista toward my childhood home. At a tennis court on the high school campus, a young man and woman looked up at us and wanted to catch us to make money. So my friends and I teased this fellow, getting very close and then dashing away. But the man made a tiny lasso with a string and it caught me by the ankle. I just laughed. I wasn't afraid, and my friends flew on, unworried.

But I played along with the guy. He took me and closed me up in his garage, where I met two other regular humans he had imprisoned, a mother and a boy about five. I told them not to worry; we would soon be free. I then proceeded to trick the man into coming out to the garage again. When he opened the door, I slipped by him and called the police. The police came to arrest the fellow, while the mother and son told the officers their story. I was allowed to go free because of fairy law, which said that I didn't have to get involved with human law.

The ending of the dream was completely unexpected. I found myself as myself, sitting with Phil at an outdoor café table in San Diego near the ocean. I could see my fairy self flying into town, and then I saw a handsome naked fairy man fly up to join her, and they began to make love in the air. He was Oberon, the King of the Fairies! Phil and I both thought what a wonderful way to make love, so free and wild, and we laughed and looked at each other meaningfully.

Some dreams, like this one, follow me into my day life for a long time. Somehow this dream started me on a plan to be free. I saw that my inner being could live a life of joy and freedom while still helping others. I didn't need to get involved in all the customs, reports, all the rigamarole of taking care of a human situation. I was separate. Fairies live by fairy law which is based on mischief, selfishness, and joy;

as a fairy, I came first.

Imagining the fairy helped me as I continued to deal daily with Phil's hospitalization, his halfway house period, and then the boarding house details when he felt better and could be on his own. I was still my loving human self, doing too much for my body, but carrying on, but the fairy inside me cheered almost wickedly each time I said no to Phil's dragging need to go back to how it was before.

The boarding house was a big old Victorian house near downtown Reno. Old trees grew on a bumpy lawn where a darling mini black pug frolicked; I always had to give that pup a hug. Then the landlord, who kept a close eye on his dog, would come out of his adjoining little house to say hi. This young man was lanky, with floppy black hair, and an energetic way about him. He tried to get all the guys renting the rooms into a social circle of activities, which I think sometimes worked when there was food involved. Phil's room was upstairs next to a shared bathroom. He had a bed, chair, desk, a window crowded close with tree leaves outside.

Phil didn't like his room at first. He wanted to come home. He said he was lonely and wanted to be with me, but I discovered there was a sneakier sadder reason in his mind: that if he kept the room, he would have to pay the rent, and if he used his money for rent, he wouldn't have enough for a trip. I saw this sneaky reason early on in our adjustment to having two places. In fact, I soon realized that it was the solution. Project Oberon had a solution! Keep paying his rent on the room!

So each month on the 3rd, we would take the rent check to the manager across the street. A big chunk, maybe 300 was taken out of Phil's 800 disability payment. That left him the slimmest budget for cigarettes and food and forced him to consider living through the days of the month instead of pursuing the amazing future of his daydreams. Even so, twice Phil attempted to escape by privately giving the manager notice, telling her he planned to leave the next month. But she called me, and I said, no, he wasn't leaving; we'd pay the rent as usual. Then I took the rent check over myself. Somehow this strategy worked without Phil getting too upset.

Still, Philly, my man, resisted Project Oberon with many tired complaints and mean jabs. The therapist said that was Phil testing my boundary. Would I hold? I did, but it was just as hard for me; we were lonely for each other, wanting the best of us being together, and it hardly seemed right to keep us apart.

But Phil did well despite himself. He started walking around the neighborhood, taking the local bus places, talking to some of the other guys. We talked on the phone, of course, multiple times a day and I drove into town often, too. I came to love visiting him. It reminded me of our days of first courtship, how I'd come into his single room smiling, hugging, and then we'd talk or settle on the bed to play around. Now it was 20 years later, yet I was still in love, and he was still in love, too. We didn't play in bed, but that was coming soon. Yes! I didn't know - so it was a big surprise when Phil said we could make love again. Maybe the Fairy King Oberon spoke to him about it in a dream. But I'm getting ahead of my story.

I'd sit in his boarding house room while he puttered at making coffee, and I noticed how tall, how much a man, Phil looked as he stood above me. That was one of the pros of Phil living separately. He became a man again in my mind because I wasn't worrying about him as much. I wasn't taking on his care as much, like a mother would. Though he fought like a bucking wild horse as he resisted the boundary I'd tied him to, gradually he calmed into himself and began feeling independent and capable again.

Debbie Bumstead

❧The Romance of Portola ❧
2007 Memories

In 2002 our little Boston Terrier, Bridget had died, a great loss of joy around the place. A few months later Phil and I drove out toward Pyramid Lake to a ranch where a couple had two sets of Border Collie mix pups from one mother; some had an Australian Cattle Dog dad, the others a brown Doberman. Most of the puppies' tails had been docked, yet I wanted one with a tail, so I only had a couple to choose from. The first I chose was a odd-looking brown "Borderman" the ranch lady called her, but then the woman dug into the den and brought out a bright white puppy with muted black spots from the cattle dog pups, and she had a whippy tail. I decided on her instead because her eyes were dark and lovely. As we drove home, I said to Phil, "Let's call her Jenny! Just for my best friend in second grade." Jenny the pup was trouble from the start. She was so growly, jump-uppy, wild and shy, I tried to give her back! How often I've wondered what kind of dog I'd have had if I'd kept the Borderman!

When I finally accepted the challenge of owning Jenny, I began a schedule of taking her to different places to be socialized with people and other dogs. One summer's day Phil and I took her and drove to Portola, a small town in California north of our place and famous in my family because this was the town my mom's family moved to from Alabama in the 1930s. Her uncles and then her father had found jobs at the Box Factory near Portola, and my mom had gone to high school there before moving to Reno. Because of Mama's memories, which I'd heard all my life, Portola had a nice old historical aura all its own inside me. Phil liked it because of the pine woods and mountain air, as we toured around town.

With Jenny lying in the back seat cowering, we drove by the movie theater, which Mama had worked at all those many years ago, and down the old town and then up into very old residential streets. This area charmed me. The little houses were so close and small, they must have been company houses at one time for the factory or sawmill, I thought. The present owners of these tiny places had decorated their porches and yards with many bright windsocks or tinkling wind chimes or other jaunty doodads. I liked this cheery style so much, I bought windsocks and chimes for our house, too, after we came home.

We bought snacks at the store and took Jenny to a park near a lake, where she perked up and played Frisbee with me. Jenny loved Phil from the beginning. She looked on him, as I did, as the leader of our pack, and like I did, she leaned on him, wanted his hands on her, and gazed at him with her ears back! Yes, Jenny and I were alike in our shyness and our need for a hero, and she needed taming just as I had. I still have her, 12 now, and, like me, some improved, but not much. I remember getting very crabby after hiking in the Portola park with Jenny; I was so achy I wanted to go home suddenly. How kind Phil was as we headed back; he really was very patient with me, more so than I was with him, I do believe. But maybe not - maybe he was patient in the day to day, and I was patient in the long run.

***

But now it was 2007 and Phil and I had both lost patience with the other. It took some time for us to settle down, as Phil's mental health improved and I calmed my nerves with the separation. Then we began to fudge a little on my boundary. Not really, but my therapist in our discussion one week said maybe it wouldn't hurt for Phil stay the night with me sometimes. He would still have the room to live in most of the time, but since we both missed each other in the evenings, why not have him over. This plan worked for us, but sometimes Phil balked at coming over, he said to show me that he "could take a stand" too.

Then Phil's name came to the top on a list for a studio in a nice apartment building near the hospital. It was freshly painted, clean, with a kitchen and bathroom. Phil's family helped furnish it with a comfy green plaid chair and ottoman, a twin bed, and even though he wasn't a big television fan, a TV on a neat stand went into his new home. He liked the place, and I loved it. Very often I daydreamed I could just move in with him and live a very simple life in one room with just us two, no yard, no dogs and cats (but maybe just one or two), no stuff to take care of. Like our interlude in San Diego in the studio of an old Victorian house, we would have ourselves alone to care for and entertain in the big beautiful world around us.

This, I believe, would have been a solution for us both, and perhaps we should have been independent from the beginning like grown-ups are supposed to be. But my family was intertwined inside me so much I was stuck, too weak to break away. With my Grandmother and then my Mama providing our housing to keep us near and paying emergency bills through the years, it was easy to give in and be dependent on them. Now my mom needed my company and care, and I still needed her for housing and big bills; besides, I liked her and loved her, and could never abandon her. Given that, Phil and I couldn't try the solution of being independent. Probably wouldn't work for long anyway; we'd tried it before. The year we lived on our own in a rented condo and the year we worked for Phil's parents' furniture store in Gridley were both favorite times of mine, but they ended when Phil's mind took a downward turn.

But I saw the other solution now, though I never voiced it to Phil. Simply, my plan (part of Project Oberon) was to always pay the rent on Phil's separate residence with part of his monthly check. To pay it even if Phil stayed at the house with me for several days or even all week. Keeping the room solved the traveling problem for Phil for the rest of his life - he never again had enough money to take a trip!

***

By saving my own money in bits I had enough for a trip myself, and I invited Phil to a weekend in a fancy lodge near Portola, old Portola again. For all the time that Phil had been sick with his mental health issues, I had taken on the driving when we went around town together. But Phil was better, so on our vacation, and like in the past on our road trips, Phil took the wheel and drove us. I liked that. It made me feel like Phil was in charge again. I was tired of being in charge. He was a man again, now with his own place, now driving the freeway north in our maroon van, now free of our families, except that my mom was home taking care of Jenny this time and the other pets for us.

Easy drive, empty countryside, sunshine, patches of snow - we drove up Highway 395 alongside the Long Valley creek. My mom had often told me of her fear of drowning here. In the 40s the road followed the stream closely, and when she drove from Portola where she was still living with her grandma to finish up high school to Reno where her parents were now working and living, she was afraid, as a new driver, that she'd run off the pavement into the water. There was another drowning story that happened in the same time - Mama's Uncle Clarence drowned in the East River in New York, having fallen out of a rowboat on his birthday into the cold waves. These thoughts made my mind see this area as haunted with death by drowning. And the further story of Uncle Clarence, who had earlier ditched the Army, and then changed his name to Pierce Stradley so as not to get caught (and hanged?) was so mysterious I told Phil about it as we zipped along.

"Who changes his name from Clarence Duncan to Pierce Stradley?" I asked. "Where did he hear such a name? It sounds like a character in a book."

The strangest part is how a simple creek bed passing outside the windows of a car can jog memories that aren't even mine firsthand, and whole stories can wisp around in the air taking in more than the present time and space, spreading from Alabama, New York, Portola, wartime home front, and all. And then to exist there, in our present as Phil and I chatted on our vacation trip, and beyond, to now, as 2016 begins, Phil's been dead seven years and I sit in our Aldebaran House by my patio door, my dog PJ (Phil's Jasper) like a golden curly rug at my feet. It all fits together, but who can take the trouble to care, except for me, as I conjure up all the memories of our last vacation? I don't know how I stand this hardness of Nature. And to know the beauty, too, mixed in? I only cope because I can't argue. Nature is like death, even though death is a part of Nature; just as I can't argue with death, I can't argue with Nature. Or maybe I mean Physics.

At the Portola Junction where 395 met up with 70, we turned and followed the highway bordered by long sweeps of pasture land and ranches. Our Lodge was past the old town of Portola actually, almost to the edge of an upscale town named Graeagle. The lodge made me think of hunting lodges famous in European novels, surrounded by trees, faced with dark hills and close to snow-topped mountains. The lobby looked rich to our poor eyes with its big fireplace and all the tables and chairs, and our room seemed even better since the huge bed was covered with a duvet (as the brochure called it) that fluffed up around us as we plopped down for a rest. That duvet was luxurious, and I noticed it throughout our stay, planning to get one for our bed at home, maybe in light yellow, like a cloud it would be on a sunny day. The lodge duvet was plain dark brown and under it were high count sheets of cream color all smooth and clean.

Did I have an intuition that this would be our last road trip? I don't think so, but I felt full of happiness and energy that day, out with my old pal, just well from his bout with the mind's illness, ready to be his own self again. He was kind, cheerful, and eager to give me whatever I wanted to do on our trip as a gift. Did I want to visit the little shops? We stopped at one, and I bought a garden stake of metal in the shape of a kooky lady frog. Did I want lunch at the café? Should we buy some treats for later in our room? We did every little thing I wanted, and then we drove around the newer area of Portola across the highway from the old town where we'd explored last time. Phil liked the ranch style homes in their expansive yards with tall pine trees growing dark and green, so he began daydreaming of living there. And I was expansive enough to indulge his daydream, even though I was now perfectly happy with Aldebaran House. How good it could have been, though, he as a man, buying his wife a home in the forest, where they might live all alone together again.

There is a part of me that might have been the largest happiest me if only, if only. No one has seen this part of me for long, though I think some people have noticed it hiding in my words and actions and liked me for it. Only Phil got to see this complete person, and for our last vacation I had two days of being that Debbie. It felt good - like a combination of a girl child with her father to herself and a woman with her longtime loving man, added to the lover with joy sprouting out all over. No, it wasn't that excessive, but anyway, I was happy. We came back to our room at the Lodge in the afternoon to rest, read, wander around outdoors, and talk.

We drove further north to a fancy steakhouse for dinner - money was no object! Back in the room, we watched a movie, about Bruce Willis having to take a witness across town to court to testify against a bad guy, who was determined to kill the witness before they got there. It was the kind of action movie which Phil enjoyed, though at the same time disliked for its violence. Afterwards we watched a softer movie, something like *The Secret Garden*, which we both liked.

The lushness, the beauty, the blooming and blossoming flowers of my own secret place, though, lay unvisited that night. I asked Phil to make love, but he only hugged me to him, kissed me good-night, and I had to pull away when he quickly fell asleep and began to snore. Over to the other side of the big bed I went, snug like a lonely little animal in her den under the smooth sheets and fluffy duvet.

***

Now, as a foreshadowing of the future, I must mention a problem Phil had most of his life, which I, and really he, too, just took in stride for years - his constipation. He took several medications that added to the problem, and though he had tried many different methods of relief, he still had bad days of bloating and pain before taking his desperate cure, which was a lot of suppositories all at once up his bottom. When Phil woke up the second day of our vacation with pain in his abdomen, he sat on the edge of the bed, leaning uncomfortably to ease the pain, his expression that wince that showed when he didn't feel well. He wanted to sleep in and take it easy.

"I'm going to try the complimentary breakfast," I said. "I'll bring you some coffee." I dressed and wandered alone to the Lodge lobby where a busy buffet was set out for everyone. I liked sitting at a table in a room with a long many-paned window looking out over the golf course under the pine trees. First a couple about my age, but much more elegant than Phil and I, struck up a chat with me. When they left, a single woman in her forties probably, began to tell me about her job, traveling around the western states, staying in various hotels and motels. She was a new sales representative, just getting used to it, but she felt lonely a lot. We talked easily, as if we could have been friends, if we'd had more time. I told her Phil was waiting for a roll and some coffee, but later in the morning, as Phil suffered on in the room, I wandered out again onto the bright crisp day and sat with the single woman again near the fire-pit to talk some more. How often I've thought of her since then, wondering if things went well for her. I don't know if I would have recognized her again, seems she was shorter than I, dark-haired, maybe a little plump, as I was; I don't know if we even exchanged first names. Hello, wherever you are!

Soon, I was back in the room packing up our stuff, while Phil was in the bathroom. When we were ready to leave, we lay down on the big bed again until check-out time. I pulled the duvet up over us and soothed Phil's temples with my fingers by stroking his silky red curls. It was hard for him after his bathroom visits, too, as all the work of pooping strained muscles and mind, as well. It was a problem Phil suffered through without much complaint, so we neither of us realized how it would lead to such drastic consequences and tragedy within a couple of years. Phil was feeling better about 10:30, enough that we visited the lobby for his breakfast, before he took the wheel again, and we drove off together, together.

Back home, out of romantic Portola, where my mom's youth and my own womanliness lived comfortably inside me, we went. It was the Town of the Portal, you might call it, where history and present day lead to the whole of me, a human being.

❧Making Love Again ❧
2007 & 2008 Selected Journal Entries

June 16, 2007 - Saturday - Hot

Phil put on the record with Keith Caradine singing "I'm Easy," and it was so pretty Phil said, "I wish I could feel the love I have for you like this even when the music ends." I told him I knew exactly what he felt, that music seemed to connect with emotion and so made emotion more understandable and pure. I said that it happens in my dreams, too, my emotions are so strong and pure and more than anything can be in real life.

June 19, 2007 - Tuesday - Hot

On Sunday when Phil put "I'm Easy" on again, I told him I wasn't feeling well enough to listen to it, but he said he'd just play it a couple of times. After it played I said, "I wish you were as easy as the man in the song." I began to cry really hard. Phil went out to smoke, so I let myself feel such sadness about Phil not wanting to make love anymore. I just let my feelings overpower me and sobbed. Phil came back in and said, "Why don't you come sit by me and let me help you." So I sat by him with his arm around me. I cried that he didn't want to help me like I needed to be helped. He rubbed my arms with his warm hands. He told me he loved me for helping the children, for going to the pool and making friends with the ladies, for going to therapy; he loved how I tried and did things. But I cried that I wanted to be together again. He said, "You'll see in the future why we don't need that now, but for now I guess I can't help you." Then I just cried and he rubbed my arm and my back and squeezed me to him.

Then today with my therapist I told her about this episode, and we talked about a lot of things. She said the men in my life had been in control of my sex life from Uncle Hersey's molesting me to my dad's breaking up with my mom to my high school boyfriend's sexless-ness, and now to Phil and having to accept his way or no way. She wondered if Phil's rigid no to sex means he can't give me some things I need without full intercourse, like touching and so forth. Then we talked about self-stimulation and she said there were many ways to experiment with that. I told her sometimes I do that kind of thing, but always feel sad it isn't Phil.

July 21, 2007 - Saturday - Sunny

Things feel changed this week. First I got tired of being sad and told myself to stop. That's made me feel better for a couple of days, even when I did have a sad feeling go by. Then the other thing that happened is very private, and even if this is just for me, it's a little embarrassing to put down. Anyway I took my therapist's suggestion and got a massager by mail order and used it yesterday to stimulate myself (when Mama was at the Senior Center and I was alone). It felt good, and physically just like Phil making love to me. I enjoyed it so much that somehow I felt sure Phil would understand and maybe get stimulated himself if I told him. But though he accepted it all right as I talked to him on the phone, the subject made him sad and sorry for me. Later he called back and told me that he'd decided he won't come over anymore, that we could still be friends, but we're too different. He said it wasn't because of "what you did," but just that we're too different. I was very hurt and angry, and didn't say anything. I haven't spoken to him since.

I thought to myself, "He'll change his mind, he always does." But then I felt angry. He makes me feel like I'm dirty for wanting him, like my sexuality is poison to him. Though he loves me, hugs me, kisses me, and though we cuddle up in bed, as soon as I want the least bit more intimacy, he shies away and runs and calls back disapproving words that make me feel wrong. The way he disapproves and pulls back hurts me more than the fact that maybe he can't have sex. Because I realize he may be physically unable and that's OK. But to push me away like I'm dirty hurts.

Also I haven't changed. I've been this way all our marriage, enjoying the physical side of it and loving his manliness. So it isn't like I'm suddenly different.

So that's how my days have been going. Suddenly when I became sick of sadness, I felt better and better inside as I told myself to leave it behind. Then getting angry at Phil for treating me like a leper has probably helped me stand up for myself inside.

July 24, 2007 - Thunderclouds

I had a good talk with my therapist about the changes. I told her how Phil said we were too different and he didn't want us to stay overnight anymore. She wondered what brought it on, and I said I was too embarrassed to tell her. But then I did end up telling her about the self-stimulation thing, how it made me so happy I felt like I could tell Phil, but he was revolted and made me feel dirty. My doctor told me in a healthy relationship the partner who wasn't able to have sex would be supportive of that action to fill my need, that it was OK to take care of myself. She advised me that if Phil brought up the subject, asked if I'd thrown away the massager or something, to set a boundary and not talk about it. She said it was good that I'd gotten angry because he had torn something inside me by saying those things. I cried and said I missed the side of Phil that was loving and warm and sexual.

"Oh, My Redwood Heart!"

My therapist said my sexual urges were normal for a married woman my age. That it was very difficult for me to have led a life in which men either subjected me to unwanted sexual activities (Uncle H molesting me, Dad being oversexed) or didn't give me all I needed (my high school boyfriend and Phil.) I was never in control of my own sex life.

July 30, 2007 - Monday - Hot
Phil did bring the subject up once last week on the phone. He said he wished I'd throw away that "porn thing." I said it wasn't a porn thing and I didn't think we should talk about it. He said I shouldn't need it, that men were for that. I said I didn't have a man to fill that need and didn't plan on looking for one. I said, "I wish you could understand." I think that tripped some nice understanding in his mind, because he said, "I do understand. I used to do that self-stimulation myself."

Then he seemed to let it go, and we were good together again. He came over Saturday morning and I will take him home tomorrow.

August 14, 2007 - Wednesday - Hot
This afternoon my moods have been up then down. I took a rest about 2 and then woke up ½ hour later and lay there lazily reading a gothic romance. I felt like my old self and it was good. I got up and took a walk with Jenny for 10 minutes and watched some TV. I called Phil. Now I feel downhearted. I wish I wasn't so interested in having sex with him again. I guess I do because it made Phil and me so sweet together. I want the exciting feelings of love back. How close we were, how free, how sexy and exciting. I want it so badly, but I feel I have no chance of getting Phil to understand and want it, too. I think the only way to keep Phil in my heart is to realize it might be that it isn't really a choice with him to have or not have sex. He is mentally and probably physically

unable to, and that's why he doesn't even try. In other words, he would love me if he were well enough.

So I have to learn not to expect him to change or get well. I have to learn to get along happily without physical love. It's not my choice, but it is reality.

August 27, 2007 - Monday - Hot
I remembered my thoughts about keeping Phil in my heart when he was over today and we had the same old fuss. He said some mean things to me, and I said some mean things, too. But then I went to Phil's side on the couch and said I was sorry, that I wanted to be friends, that I was sorry I brought up sex all the time. "But I want it so badly," I cried on his chest. Phil rubbed my arm, said he was sorry he couldn't help me. I thought, is it all my fault? I can't figure it out. Is life trying to teach me a lesson? Or is it all chance? Or is it all a rock slide started by Uncle Hersey?

***

Star! October 12, 2007 - Friday - Cold and Cloudy *Star!*
Wow, what a change in Phil on Wednesday. I keep smiling to myself about it. Phil decided to help me with my sexual desires! What in the world changed his mind! Did I wear at him so much, he took pity on me? Did my purchase of the "thing" waken his mojo? Or was it the sneaky tease I gave him a week or so ago when we were on the phone, me at home, he at his apartment - I teased, "Maybe if you made love to me every week again, I'd let you move back here." Of course in my mind at the time, I was also thinking, "but I'll keep paying your room rent!" Oh, my funny Phil.

So, when he was home this week and I came to bed Wednesday, not knowing yet that he'd decided this, I asked if he'd hold me. He said yes. Then I asked if I could leave off my PJs and he said yes. So when I lay next to him, he gently began caressing my breasts. I was so surprised and happy that I was immediately aroused, and the more he touched me the more aroused I became. We kissed, too. I was so excited I turned to hug and told him, "I wish you could go inside me," but he said "I'm sorry, I can't yet." I burst into tears and buried my head in his chest. He rubbed my back and told me to relax and gradually I did. I told him thank you for helping me like this, and he said he knew I needed it and he could help me just a little.

During the night when I'd wake up, I'd smile to myself. Thursday we laughed and talked about it a little. I asked him if he felt pleased like I did, and he said he was pleased that he could help me.

***

March 12, 2008 - Wed. - Mild
Phil and I have been together sexually on and off many times, since last fall - amazing that I haven't even kept count. Like, yesterday evening he touched me a little and I him, but he was so sleepy it didn't last long. Still I woke up this morning contented and seeing him in a bright light. His manliness is an essential part of my regard for him, and being intimate, even briefly, makes him more a man to me.

Wish he could see that. I think it helps him as much as it does me, if he'd only acknowledge it. We are friendlier to each other through our days together, and forgive irritations more easily. And the strange thing is that when I have enough intimacy in my life, the importance and obsession of it calms down in my mind, and the subject doesn't seem so overwhelmingly constant.

March 20, 2008 - Thursday - Sunny
Last night after Phil touched me awhile and then we relaxed together, all warm and naked in each other's arms, I

had the strangest feeling, the feeling of liking the moment, of being completely there, with no ambitions or plans or worries. It was beautiful.

March 26, 2008 - Wed.

Hurray, I got to say "No," a couple nights ago. Phil and I've been getting together in bed each evening for a week. Yes, every night for a week, instead of once weekly as we did previously in our marriage. Well, one night I was so sleepy, I actually told Phil, "I think I'll just go to sleep tonight." He made a disappointed sigh, but we turned to our sides and slept, and today I'm thinking of all the many times I had to initiate or beg for sex, and the other many times Phil would ask for sex and I'd hop right to it, never refusing him, even in the middle of the night when he had to wake me. But this one time, I got to feel I'd had enough, and I got to say, "Not tonight."

⚡A Strong Man ⚡
2008 Memories

In his last year of life, Phil gave me that kindest gift of a resurgence of physical love. How sweet, and how I loved him for at last giving me more of the healing touches I needed so much in my life. But while Phil took time for my needs, he also survived three near-death illnesses in 2008. The first, in January, was double pneumonia, discovered after Phil fell down at a bus stop in town and was taken to the hospital. He had been on his own at his apartment a few days, so I was shocked when I got the phone call. When I came to Phil's side in the hospital, he could hardly speak, but he held my hand and we were glad to smile at each other. The doctor told me in the hallway that Phil had not only pneumonia, but infections in his gall bladder, liver, and pancreas. "We'll take out his gall bladder as soon as he is stronger," the doctor told me. This, the doctor thought, might be what was causing Phil's intestinal troubles, too. It sounded as if Phil could be getting better in time.

But none of them took into account his mental health. I warned the nurses about his mental state on my second or third visit because I sensed Phil's mind was beginning to falter. I asked if he was getting his mental health meds, and the nurse told me the doctor thought it better not to right now. "He'll get worse in his thoughts," I warned her. It was only when a day or two later Phil began to struggle to leave the bed and couldn't see reason that the nurses got the message and made the doctors notice. Every single time Phil was hospitalized, I had to remind them about giving him his mental health meds, because they, for reasons of their own about his physical health, wouldn't think it necessary, and every single time, after a couple of days, the nurses had to urge the doctors to act, after seeing themselves and having to deal with what Phil was like when he was getting psychotic.

Another problem caused by Phil's mental illness cropped up when Phil was transferred to a rehab hospital to recover and go through lots of tests to decide how to continue his treatment, which would include an operation. Phil stayed a day or two there, but as he had when he suffered from the empyema, he refused the operation. He wanted to come home right away, now. I tried hard to talk him into staying, seeing it through. But he turned mean in his effort to get free.

It was so strange. There we were in his room, a nurse and doctor and I, explaining how he needed to find out what was going on in his body and take care of it, or he would die. I begged him and firmly ordered him, either way, he said no over and over again, and the doctor's words didn't convince him. When the nurse said he should stay for his wife's sake, Phil acted so cold about me, it hurt me to the core. He said things like I didn't have control of him, I didn't know what was best, and he didn't care if I was hurt or not. In Phil's mind he would say anything to get his freedom from that scary place, and so it was: he couldn't be forced to stay. He was dressed and ready to go, his expression and words still hard as I followed along down the hospital hallway to the lobby door.

And then - like a switch, as soon as we got outside and into our van, he was suddenly calm and kind, his normal self! I realized that he had been putting on an act! Though deep down perhaps his mental health **was** causing him to fear an operation, he had actually been making up his anger at me and the others to get his way. As soon as he got his way, he turned back into my nice old guy, Phil! It was such a shocking realization, I laughed. Though I was embarrassed for his behavior and lost some respect for him, I was glad because his act meant all his hard words had been said to an end, not as a truth.

***

He came home, and as with the empyema, he had tubes and pills to help him live awhile longer. As before, he got better. But not very. He continued to have digestive trouble, and he lost weight because he didn't feel like eating. His stomach hurt. One morning in April he walked into the kitchen and simply fell down; he didn't know why. He got up, saying no to my suggestion to see the doctor, and a few minutes later he fell down again. My mom and I urged him to go to the emergency room, and he finally agreed.

As I drove him to town, he sat holding his stomach and groaning - his stomach was blowing up like a big balloon. When we reached the VA Hospital, the doctors and nurses hurried him in without the usual wait, and I was called in to join him quickly. We were told Phil would be transferred to the other hospital where they had better equipment. As Phil and I waited for the paperwork, we sat together holding hands. Phil was well in his mind, though his face was contorted in pain, and he calmed me more than I him. Phil told me the doctor said he had a blockage in his intestine and also that his heart was beating irregularly. I saw a tube sticking into him that was draining some awful green liquid out of his stomach into a container.

Then I saw him briefly in the emergency room at the other hospital, where doctors and nurses prepared him for surgery. His dark eyes sparked at me in the whiteness of the room around us.

"I love you, Debbie," he said.

"I love you, Phil," I said.

187

Debbie Bumstead

Then I drove my aching self home, not really realizing how serious Phil's journey was going to be. In surgery the doctors found part of his intestine was necrotic (dead!), and they had to remove some of it. He also had a heart attack, they told me over the phone.

When I drove in the next day, Phil was in the ICU connected to a breathing machine. The doctor didn't expect him to live out the day. I sat beside his bed for a few hours, crying and being calm both. I just held his hand and stared at him, his closed eyes, his beard bristly chin, his red eyebrows. It seemed like I couldn't get enough of Phil being still alive, like his aliveness needed to be photographed by me.

The next day Phil's heart began to recover, beating more strongly. The next day he had a second operation, closing up his abdomen after taking out the gall bladder. The doctor told me it may have been the gall bladder which caused the whole problem as there was a hole in it. Days passed, and soon Phil opened his eyes briefly and seemed to hear us talking to him. He also grimaced when the nurses changed his position in the bed. Each day I felt more hopeful. Was he going to beat death once more? The pain on his face, though, made me think about how he would be suffering the recovery process. But he'd be alive. I hoped he'd be glad to be alive.

Then the day came when Phil talked to me. I told him I loved him and he said, "Ah Uh Oo" back. I told him about his operation. I asked him questions and he seemed to answer them, though I couldn't understand his noises. He said "Ah Uh Ooo" again and I said "I love you, too, Phil." I'm very sure he said that. Eight days after his operation, Phil awoke fully. When I went in to say hi to him that day, he opened his eyes to look at me and we both smiled ear to ear.

"I'm so glad to see you awake, so glad to see your beautiful eyes!" I told him.

He still couldn't talk because of the breathing machine tube; instead he nodded and shook his head to my questions.

But though he became more alert and active as time went on, he seemed very nervous, clinching his hands and frowning and moving his legs around. I was afraid once again he was feeling his mind's trouble. At my question, the nurse said she thought that that day they would start his mental health meds, but again it took days more for the doctors to catch on.

On the morning Phil came off the breathing machine, it was great to hear him talk. But, poor man, he was still not in his right mind and as usual he wanted out of the hospital right away! He complained to the nurses that he was starving, not understanding that a tube was feeding his stomach. A restraint around his chest kept him in bed - I sat with him an hour being chipper and feeling kind of happy despite his complaints.

He was moved to a slightly lower acute care area in the hospital, but he still wasn't doing very well psychologically. The nurses told me one night he tried to get out of bed for hours. I felt so sorry that Phil couldn't come out of the disorientation, though even as his was, he was sweet and confused, not belligerent, and the nurses liked him. But his intelligence or clear sight wasn't there, and I felt helpless. As usual, I wanted to reach into his mind and turn on the sharp side.

But then, finally, finally, the doctors smartened up and gave him some Haldol to help his mind. Though this wasn't his normal mental health medicine, he calmed down and became more alert and talkative again. So my spirits went up. He looked very thin, and had lost his muscles, so his next step in recovery was to be transferred to a rehab place to get stronger.

That last day at the hospital before moving to rehab, Phil told me, "You are going to make my last days good."

I replied, "I hope you are going to live longer than that."

And he said, "I might live a week, a month, or five years."

To be exact he lived four more months.

Debbie Bumstead

***

After some days of positive steps toward being able to walk and exercise in the rehabilitation hospital, Phil's health took another dive. He was weak, his stomach ached and he had painful gas. I felt cross with his treatment, since I had thought the stomach and gas problems would go away after the gall bladder infection cleared. Why couldn't things be easier for him? I wished if he had to die soon that it wouldn't be painful and hard. Dear one.

Almost daily I sat with him, talked with and teased him in his huge single room with a window looking out on our parked car. When he couldn't make it to the exercise room, he tried at least to sit in the recliner next to his bed. I see him now, pensively looking out on the sunny day, at the Dairy distributing building across the street - did it remind him of his ranch days as a youth, riding horses and rounding up cattle? I'd tap on the open door, he'd turn his face to me, smile sweetly, happy for my company. Sometimes we closed the door part way and sat together in the raised bed, close, warm, his left palm resting on my thigh. Dearest one.

Of course Phil wanted out of there desperately, and he spent some wasted time complaining to the nurses and threatening to get a lawyer. Meanwhile he was having constipation and then terrible diarrhea with messy accidents in the bathroom, and though I felt compassion for him, I wondered how it would be if he came home. Still later, when I was at home by myself, while lying on our big pillowy bed, a breeze blew the curtains like in my dream, and my Willy cat came around to purr near me, and I suddenly thought, "I can't take care of Phil. I can't." What was I to do? If I thought of Phil and my love for him, I knew it would be all right somehow. But then circumstances were sure to come up - mainly, if Phil got stubborn, or refused to cooperate, or hurt me with his words. Just as I rested there, the phone rang. It was Phil, nauseated and in great pain. "Oh, God," he whispered over and over again, unable to say more. My man, my man, was he going to die soon? Why was he suffering so much? Dear heart.

I almost hate to write what next happened. Yes, Phil came home and we had quiet simple days of happiness together for a week or so. Home nurses came to care for him, while he was able by himself to go to the bathroom, out to smoke on the patio, and to eat a little bit. But after a horrible accident of poop on the rug in front of the bathroom, it was too much for him, and me, too. As I cleaned up, Phil sat on the edge of the bed, completely weakened and helpless. Another few days and again his stomach swelled, his heart quickened, and the ambulance took him to the hospital and he ended up in ICU after another operation. Oh, heartless Nature!

But this time Phil surprised us all by waking up perky and friendly. I was amazed and happy when I went into Phil's room at the Veteran's Hospital ICU and found him awake, bright-eyed, alert, kind, happy, feeling pretty good. The nurse said he had had a blockage due to adhesions and hopefully that's fixed now. I thought, how wonderful if it were so, and I felt lighter inside at his new wellbeing. Later, though, I was a little afraid because I thought of something I had read that one possible stage of dying was to rally and feel better for awhile. Still, Phil was amazing, to go so low and then to revive again time after time. When I called the hospital the next morning, the nurse told me he was doing even better, and that he was cute and she liked him.

Makes me loathe to add that a few days later, he again came down with pneumonia. #*!#! (Your favorite cuss word)

But - he recovered from that as well, and came home to me for another couple of weeks. How can one believe it?

❦Broken Wing ❧
Memories & Journal Entries - June-August 2008

One night in June around nine, Phil fell as he was walking to the table. He was weak from not eating. I couldn't lift him, and didn't know how else to help, since he said he didn't want to go to the hospital. Then his sister phoned while he was down and suggested I call a neighbor, so the neighbor man and his son came over and got Phil up into the wheelchair. When they left, I still didn't know what I could do to help. I felt we were just putting off the inevitable trip to the hospital. Phil somehow crawled out of the chair onto the bed. He slept all night, but in the morning he had so much pain in his leg, I knew we had to call the ambulance.

So there he was at the VA again. Both bones in the lower part of his leg were broken, but the doctors didn't want to operate until later, due to his previous heart attack. He had instead to live in their nursing home unit, in a building connected to the hospital. Phil's spirits were fair, but mine were low at first. If Phil's dying, I wondered to myself, why must he suffer on and on? I guess that's the way life and death are, I tried to tell myself, and soon it will be my turn, but for now, I must go on, too. That second evening at home I was lonely and sad; how much more would happen to my loved one?

But I woke up feeling better, even energetic. I set out to clean up the house and do laundry, and then sat down to do some writing. It helped to remember something my psychologist had said about turning my thoughts from feeling like I'm being assaulted by all these calamities to looking at how well I deal with them, how strong I've been, how efficiently I've gotten Phil help, how well I do at crying when sad, but perking up when the crying is over.

So began a couple of months of visiting Phil at the nursing home. Sometimes, at first, he was so sleepy we hardly talked, and I wondered if he was strong enough to live any more time at all. I felt his life coming to a close, yet Phil didn't realize how dire his health was.

"Why can't I go home?" he asked the doctor, plaintively.

"Because you need help," she answered.

***

Most of the time I was lucky and got a close parking place. If I didn't, and had to cruise around the streets for some opening at the curb, life was harder for me. A long long walk, and as it was, I walked the long hall in the building to reach his room, my legs screaming as on I hobbled. But turning into Phil's room, our eyes met and the little bubble of joy that surrounded the memory of our togetherness through the years rose between us. True to his spirit, Phil revived from his sleepiness, though he was weak and couldn't get into his wheelchair very well. But when he was seated, then I took the chair handles and pushed the man of my heart out to the garden.

It was a lovely garden patio, though full of cigarette smoke as the patients puffed, sometimes with their wives sitting near them on the benches. A small fountain splashed in a square full of big blooming rosebushes, and the sun was filtered through leaves of trees that lifted to the blue sky. I don't know if other people notice this, but I have always seen the difference between my feelings when I am talking or playing or just sitting with someone I love from the feelings I have when I'm with someone I just like. It is a whole extra gob of feeling that heightens the level of the heart. That's what I felt as Phil and I enjoyed our pleasant visits by the roses. Often we spoke with others there. One wife teased Phil that he didn't know what a treasure he had in me, as I sat close by him, my arm in his. But I still felt like **he** was the treasure for me.

One day in particular I remember, I rolled him back to his room and then sat in a chair behind him and massaged his temples, his curly hair, his broad shoulders a long time in silence. It was special to me and the feeling has lasted still today, the sweet lovingness of that together time.

Phil thrived at the nursing home for a brief few weeks. He made friends of the other patients, one an older man he shared cigarettes with, who wheeled Phil down to the Canteen on days I didn't come into town. Phil also attended an arts and crafts class where he made a birdhouse from a kit. When the teacher suggested he paint the house prettily, Phil had one of his big ideas: that I would paint it using his designs, the designs that he had doodled with pen and pencil over the years, which I had kept in my file cabinet. These designs were of flowers, birds, trees, water, all done with symmetrical swirls and symbolic stripes and curlicues. They made a whimsical and bright pattern on the birdhouse. Oh, Phil, so pleased was he with this creation, he couldn't stop thanking me! The craft teacher, too, thought it lovely, entered it in a little fair, and Phil won first prize! The teacher then commissioned three more birdhouses to buy herself for her home, which Phil set me to painting with more of his pictures. Phil was thrilled to be making money with his own business at last! And I was glad to oblige, if it gave him the least bit of hope and happiness.

***

July 20 - Today's been hard on my emotions. This morning I began to cry after watching a Sesame St. film on TV about "It's all right to cry" aimed at kids. Then when I went to see Phil I cried with him and told him I wished he could come home.

July 27 - It has been a week since I wrote. How the weeks go by. Life living every minute. I'm sad right now, my eyes wet with tears. Yesterday there was a moment when I felt I couldn't cope anymore with Phil being gone from home and having to visit him. My hips and legs have been very achy from walking so much, and my shoulders from driving, pushing Phil, vacuuming and so on and on.

July 28 - I saw Phil today at the PT room. He's been able to walk a little with a walker but still seems too fragile to leave the VA. His stomach still blows up with painful gas, and his appetite is nil. Meanwhile I feel on the edge of falling apart with fear, loneliness, tiredness. The need to check out of these difficult times is so strong at moments that I've been suddenly overcome by a terrible feeling that I'm sinking and all my muscles are going to fail.

Aug 1 - I had two or three episodes of sadness today. None lasted long. But it is hard to feel the drop of my spirit. The sting of tears. The feeling that I need to lie down and get away from my life. The loneliness of not having someone - Phil - in the house with me to notice me and care. Now I've cried hard. Too hard.

***

As August went on Phil's revival faltered. He was more often unhappy, nauseas, and in pain. One day we left the building completely and sat in a picnic area at the entrance. I had brought Phil some chow mein, which he was craving, and he ate a whole plate of it, regardless of his stomach. Then I asked how I could cheer him up, so we daydreamed about how we'd buy his grandpa's old ranch in Montana. We described the cabins that'd be built, the fields planted, the horses and dogs we'd have.

"My next pet will be named Jasper," Phil said. "I like the sound of that name."

"On your horse Jasper," I told him, "and on my Dash, we will ride."

"And in the winter, we will take the RV south to escape the snow."

When I rubbed Phil's head and shoulders I felt how desperately thin he was. His stomach was swollen, though, and his legs, too. He told me that after this, he was giving up trying to eat. "I hate the laxatives they insist on giving me," he said.

I felt afraid behind my cheeriness. He isn't improving anymore, I thought; he's slowly dying. When I left him for the day, I went home, took a nap and woke up thinking, I'll never be able to hold Phil close again. He'll never be strong for me, holding me, taking care of me, just being a deep deep friend and loved one for me. I thought, he's going on another journey away from me, and this time he won't be coming back. I could always rely on Phil to come back. But now I was afraid I'd lose him forever.

The next week in my therapy session I cried and talked about my fears of Phil dying. My doctor said, "The past few months and years, you've been in practice to live without Phil as he's been gone often and ill. Now he may or may not be dying, but you must learn that you can live on without him. Will you be able to let Phil go?" she asked me.

I looked at her, considering. "I don't know if I can - yet," I said.

Downward, my Phil went. The skin on his face was suddenly lined and yellowish. The catheter hurt his penis, his testicles were swollen, and he had a terrible sore on his bottom. He was too weak to get from chair to bed anymore.

Yet he didn't think about failing at getting stronger. He talked about coming home when he could stand up and shuffle by himself. Meanwhile I continued to ask myself, can I let go of Phil? The question somehow made me feel calmer. I don't need to cling, I thought; I can live if he dies. I can let go. I knew I had believed before that I couldn't bear to be without the man who helped me grow, who was the only person I felt free with, the only person who had loved me, touched me, let me love him, touch him. But even so, I could let go - maybe, I told myself.

***

One morning I went into Phil's room at the nursing unit, and he didn't wake up for me. He smiled, but could not rouse himself. The nurses sent him back to ICU where he revived a bit. But as the week passed, Phil steadily grew more ill. Out in the hallway, the doctor told me to prepare for his passing, that the operations had not fixed something that was wrong with his system, and now, the doctor said, Phil's body was shutting down. Phil was still able to talk and listen briefly. Another morning, and Phil thought I was there to take him home. He was put out with me when I said I couldn't. But when I had to leave, I kissed him twice on the forehead, which he's always loved me to do, and he smiled and said, "You know I love you."

Those were to be his last words to me. Because the next day when I went in, he was struggling terribly for his breath, though they were giving him oxygen. He knew I was there and squeezed my hand. When Phil's sister and her husband came in from Fallon, the doctor met us to recommend that we let Phil go to comfort care, which meant the hospice room, the machines turned off, and morphine to make him comfortable.

***

Debbie Bumstead

August 29, 2008, Phil died at 9:20 in the morning. I had gotten to the VA about 8 and sat with him, holding his hand, as he lay in the comfort care room. He was completely asleep with morphine to soothe him; his breathing was very slow. Around nine I relaxed back into my chair and just kept my hand on his arm, patting it once in awhile. I looked at the art print on the wall, imagined Phil and I were walking on the path through the flowers, down to the pond, into the forest in the distance. Then I noticed how still and quiet Phil had become. He had stopped breathing so quietly, I had not noticed, and now he was gone.

❧A Fair Word From Everyone ❧
September - 2008

My brother drove my mom and me to the military cemetery in Fernley, a small town between Reno and Fallon where Phil was to be buried. Many members of his family came from different parts of the west to see him off, and we all sat in chairs in a pavilion under a sunny blue sky. The place was outside town with desert brush lying flatly to the north with low hills rising beyond. This was the desert the pioneers came through to reach California; the Donner Party had passed nearby, already in trouble before being trapped beyond Reno in the mountains. Just think of all the generations of rabbits and coyotes that had roamed here and still did! To me, it was a good place, though Phil had loved the green trees of lush landscapes, here he had nature pared down, sandy, hot in summer, cold in winter, wild, clean, and sweet-smelling.

As Phil's relatives came to hug me, I was glad for their obvious care for the unique brother, cousin, uncle that Phil had been to them. People had loved Phil throughout his life - what a wonderful thing to be able to write down - Phil was loved. I sat between Phil's sister and my mother in a softer chair someone had brought me, and I felt shy, even confused, as if the scene just couldn't be true. But then the hearse drove up, the mortuary people wheeled Phil's big casket to the front of our group, and I began to sob. Grief just washed over me like an ocean, as I had the overwhelming realization that Phil's body was in that casket. He was going to be buried. He was dead. He was gone.

There was a salute of rifles firing, and the flag on the casket was folded up and handed to me. Phil's big brother went up to the podium and told some sweet family stories, and he read a paper I had given him with messages from my mom and me:

Phil - he walks in God's garden of Love
With peace and kindness
Now and forever,
And in our memories.
He had a fair word for everyone.   Mirtle

The essence of Phil was the very best of him, and people recognized this essence right away upon meeting him. He was a gentleman. He had warmth that came through in his voice and his easy touch. He could touch people, pat them on the back, hug, take their hand, call them by name. Phil had wisdom about human emotions and understood motives good and bad. In his well times, he could apply this wisdom to himself and see his troubles for what they were. The many wise and likable and loving parts of Phil made his life beautiful and valuable to himself and to all of us he touched.

Phil gave me the greatest gift - freedom from shyness. He tamed me like the Little Prince tamed the Fox, so that for once in my life I could talk and touch and know and love completely. Phil helped me grow, gave me love, both the giving and receiving, and changed my own troubled life as I changed his. He helped me become more than I ever would have without him.   Debbie

Phil's brother-in-law gave a sermon on religious love, and after that we all had to disperse quickly since the next veteran's memorial was bumping at us. Some of us went over to the nearby building to use the restrooms, and while there, I sat on a couch at the back and watched as Phil's casket was taken to its place on the grass and buried. There was a strong pull at my heart as I saw it lowered into the ground; there goes my Phil, I thought.

Then everyone met at Fernley's restaurant for lunch, and Phil's sister, knowing me, kindly set my mother and me beside the children of the party, grand-nieces and nephews of Phil. The children perked me up, and I was glad to see also that my brother had two of my friends, who weren't so religious, to talk to.

I had made a Memory book with photos and short paragraphs about Phil's life, his jobs, his inventions in a loose-leaf notebook, and the extra pages were signed by the family and friends, some writing about their love of Phil.

*Phil was a kind uncle who always had time to talk. He was humorous and always could tell a great story.
*My love and heart for all the smiles he brought to everyone.
*I remember all the kindness he has shown me since joining the family and the humorous stories and fun ideas. He is in my heart.
*Phil was so loved. He was a kind and gentle man who will be in my heart forever.
*Phil, thanks for treating my family with love and kindness. I'm jealous that you get to see my dad (Phil's younger brother who died previously) before me. We will see you soon.
*Phil was always nice and kind. When I went to see him in the hospital all the nurses said what a nice man he was.
*Phil's memory will always be with me - much love.

***

I spent the first two weeks after the funeral at home, being quiet, crying, reading, and watching an old movie once in awhile. I got many phone calls: when I was away one day my therapist called and left a tearful message of sympathy, that's been preserved now on tape. How strange that she, my psychologist, would lose her husband, too, from a lingering illness a few years later. I kept that message as well as four from Phil when he was still at the nursing unit, trying to figure out how to get home - "having a chair that helps me stand up - that's the key.." Once in a great while I listen to these messages, still there to show me how his voice soothed the air in my ears with sweetness.

During that interval after his death I also got sympathy cards via snail mail, and several in email. My most loved friends emailed me, Debbie, my college roommate friend, Miss Kerr, my high school English teacher friend, and Denise, whom I'd met way back in 7th grade:

August 29, 2008 Oh, Debbie. I'm so sorry for your loss. But how wonderful for Phil that you were there with him to usher him on. Believe me, you will have much peace in the future because you will know that you were there and Phil had no fear or loneliness in this transition. You might be interested to know that, at the same time I was opening my e-mails to receive your message, my brother Gary called to tell me his new granddaughter was born this morning. Thank you, Phil, for making room for this new little girl. We hope she will have your gentle spirit. Much love, Debbie.

Dear Debbie: I am so saddened to hear that you now have no choice but to go on without Phil. How lucky Phil was to have you with him while he made the transition from this life. How brave of you to sit with him while he did the one thing that you dreaded most, leaving you. I cannot see you and love you with Phil's eyes; I can see you and love you with mine and I know that the specialness of you will take this sadness and grow from it, and find a way to express it and to make it a gift to others you share it with - in your own time. I am glad that you have family close. If any thought I can send you helps you to find your way, I send it gladly, reverently, with love. I will be with you in my heart tomorrow. MK

Sept.2 - It is so sad Phil left this world - the world needs all the good, kind men it can get. Isn't it wonderful that he was able to give people that knowledge that there are gentle men in the world. That is how I think of him, he left a legacy of the love that you both had for one another, and what a good person Phil was made me feel better about the world. God Bless You, Phil, and thank you for loving my friend so much. Love, Denise

Denise's message reminded me of her first impression of Phil, when she came up from California to stay with me a few days, when Phil and I were still courting. After he took us to dinner and drove us back to my place and then left, Denise exclaimed, "He certainly is a gentleman." And I'm reminded of my friend Joan's comment when she came to stay after Phil and I had been married awhile. She and I went shopping and when we got back, Phil came out to the car and began taking in the groceries, as he generally did. Joan told me, "My husband would never even think of bringing in the groceries!" That was Joan's first husband; her second is more thoughtful, I believe. I like to think, too, of the words my friends even now say about him: Miss Kerr wrote to me last time the anniversary of Phil's death came around: "I liked him because he was smart enough to love you."

In the sympathy cards I received, so many people wrote to me about their memories of Phil that I felt like his life was long, revealed, and bright. I liked one of his "J" cousin's comment I've mentioned before: "We were so sorry to hear about Phil. Our families have a long shared history and he was one of my favorite cousins. Phil was a golden boy - so cute and super smart, and great to be around and to talk to."

Uncle Glen was the father of the J cousins, and in his card he wrote that he and his wife had been traveling on the day Phil died. "On our overnight stay in Salinas on the way home from Santa Barbara Fri 29th I had a flash dream of Philip scampering around with a big smile on his face."

Another cousin from Phil's mother's side, whom I'd gotten to know in Gridley with her husband as they helped with the furniture store sometimes, wrote: "I have so many fond memories of Phil. When we visited his family in Stockton I always loved playing together. We were all close in age and had fun playing tag and jumping on the beds until our folks caught us. Philip had a little loom and he taught us how to make potholders which we took to sell to all their neighbors. I think they sold for 15 cents or 2 for a quarter. We would then head to the candy store. I always looked forward to our get-togethers with the Winans and Philip. We will miss Philip but always treasure the many wonderful memories we have of him." Funny to see that Phil had a little business, even as a child. I knew of the potholders; he'd told me the memory himself several times.

Of my family there was not so much to say. I loved the poem Mama had written the day of Phil's death, about the garden of love. My oldest brother, I think, was often irritated (as I was) with Phil's kooky inventions - Joe much preferred his own kooky inventions, and called Phil, "Phil the pill." That was all in teasy fun, of course. My other brother, Tim, was good friends with Phil, but Tim was long gone now, too, his ashes spread to the wind above a waterfall in the forest. Tim's daughters, Winter and Spring, loved Phil, I believe, along with Joe's girlfriend's daughter, all of whom spent many an afternoon with us through their growing years. Phil was a quiet presence when they came to visit; he was like a pleasant background music of smiles and soft comments behind our play.

My now grown-up niece, Winter, was at Phil's funeral, and reached forward to comfort me when I burst into tears. She wrote in her sympathy card:

Dear Aunt Debbie, All my love and hugs for you today and always. My heart goes out to you for the loss of your most special of companions, your husband. A thousand beautiful words for you and Phil could be said and more. I love you and hope for you to be able to think much on all the beauty he shared with you in your lives together and hang onto those thoughts in the days and years to come. Always remember you still have so many around you that love and care for you deeply. You're a treasure to me and I want always for you to be happy and feel at peace. With my thoughts of care to you, love, Winter

Debbie Bumstead

☙Love…A True and Wonderful Thing ☙
The 2000s - Selected Journal Entries

2000

Yesterday at suppertime Phil and I drove to the Gold Dust West to eat in their restaurant. The chairs were padded and high-backed, very fancy. The prices were low, and there was a big selection of things to eat. I got fish and chips and Phil ordered ravioli. He ate about two mouthfuls and said he was full. He has been that way all week, no appetite. I ate the delicious roll and two of my fish and some chips. Anyway it was nice to get out with Phil again. How we used to go out to casinos for meals! That is part of Phil's aura in me, the night-lighting kachunking slot machine den-like romance of casinos, even though we have only rarely gambled, just put in change sometimes. But we dated at casinos, we ate at casinos in our early marriage, and at casinos throughout our marriage. That's romance in Reno.

2001

A few days ago I came into the living room around 6, turned on the TV and saw a huge jet crash into a tall tower. I stood in awe with my mouth open for a few minutes before going to wake up Phil.

"Something is happening out in the world," I told him. "I think you'll want to see." And then went to knock at my mom's door to tell her to turn on her television. All day we all watched with the country as the terror unfolded. So hard to comprehend.

2002

I thought today that I don't do enough for Phil. He fixes his own meals, does his own laundry. The only thing I do for him is grocery shop. He drives me places, vacuums. Anyway tonight I asked him was there anything I could do. He said I could fix him some peaches.

***

My birthday went fine. I was cheerful all day. But suddenly as I did my yoga before bedtime, I began to cry. I couldn't tell why -- unless it was my hurt knee, my achiness, or the idea of getting older. I went in to be with Phil and lay with him in bed. He rubbed my back, hugged me, told me he loved me. He is my beautiful husband.

***

I've been achy, sad, impatient, and hurt most of the day. I feel physically sick almost. Tears start up whenever I stop to think what's wrong. I tried to think what was causing my sadness, but it didn't seem to have a reason, except physical aches in my arms and body. Phil just asked me how I was doing. I said, "Tears come up at odd moments."

He said, "Ahh, what's your sorrow?"

I said, tears popping up, "I don't know. I just feel so achy."

He rubbed my head with his hand.

**

Phil on another trip. I wish Phil were here. I feel so lonely for him. Life is a little boring without him around to talk to and sit by and fuss at and go places with and tell secrets to and care about. Come on, pal, come home.

2005

"I only know God, and only God knows me."

"I don't happen anymore."

"Every time he needs, he goes hungry."

"Maybe we go too far."

"Hunger and thirst after righteousness like dogs under the table."

Those are a few statements I heard when I eavesdropped on Phil's talking to himself. Some of them had more context that I couldn't hear or write down. He's been talking so much today. Joe, Mama, and I were sitting in the living room, and Phil was at the table. His talking to himself became so loud, I said, "Phil! Phil!" When he came to and said, "What?" I told him, "We can hear you." That made him laugh and I laughed with him. We both laughed so hard at the funny sad lovingness of it, that Joe and Mama joined in. Then Joe suggested he get a tape recorder and record what he says and sell the tape on eBay. I suggested using what he says to write a best-selling philosophy book.

**

Yesterday morning I felt a little afraid because Phil was talking loudly to someone imaginary named George. I asked him who George was and he said, "Never mind." He sounded angry and crazy. A little later he talked to me and said his family hated him. His dad and big brother hated him. His sister used to but she has a good heart now. Even his mom hated the things he wanted to do to get ahead. Even his little brother, Mark hated him. "But I loved Mark so much," he added, sadly, remembering Mark's death. Then he told me I was his only friend. Tears were running silently down my cheeks as he spoke. I'm glad he talked to me.

Later I got a book from the library on coping with schizophrenia. I read that schizoaffective disorder is where a person who is either depressed or manic will show schizophrenic symptoms. So I figure if Phil gets over his depression and mania the schizo stuff will go away. When I told Phil about the book, he didn't get mad. He said humorously that it was a unique sickness to have.

***

Yesterday I began to cry when I went into the kitchen to talk to Phil. He hugged me close and asked, "What's wrong?"

I cried, "Everything's wrong."

"That's how I feel," he said. I put my head against his shoulder and he hugged me. "What does your doctor say?" he asked, and I said, "She said I have to learn to accept things."

Phil asked, "What things? Me?" and I nodded. Then he said, "I wish I didn't talk out loud, but it helps my heart feel better."

I told him it was OK. It was good to be comforted by him.

***

Feeling a little sad and lonely for Phil. Why does he have to be so sick that now he must stay awhile at the Mental Health Clinic in town? (At least he is here in Reno.) Why can't he be strong and well for me? Life takes away what I love most and leaves me lonely, achy, and depressed. My heart feels as if something is pulling it out of me.

Last night I called Phil and cried awhile, and he tried to comfort me. This morning when he called, he told me nice things about me -- like I have an innocent heart which helps me say true things and feel true feelings.

2006

I'm so lonely for all the good of our marriage. Being with Phil, touching him, hugging him, sitting up close, lying down with him, telling him everything and hearing him when he's gentle and wise. I'm missing all that so much I can't be happy today. I feel dull and empty and without love.

I guess it's because Phil isn't speaking to me as if he cares. All he wants is his money in a bunch to leave.

I loved love. It felt so true and cheery and full inside me. I'm going to try to get that love back. I want to love Phil and treat him as I used to. When he sees my love, maybe his will come back, too..

***

I feel OK sometimes. Like a breeze passing over me, I feel calmness and acceptance for a brief moment. If I remember it, I am able to make it last for longer than a moment. But it is so likely to be forgotten when my loneliness or fear rush through like a wind.

If I try to remember that pretty breeze more often, maybe I'd feel better.

***

Thinking why I'm so attached to my Phil. Because Phil's the only person I've ever felt completely at ease with physically, meaning to be touched like I like to be and to touch someone back so freely like I like to do, I have only Phil. The same goes for the complete freedom I have with him to speak without shyness, without holding my emotions in check. There's nobody else I've ever been as close and free with.

That's pretty simply the reason why I cling so much to Phil or the idea of being with Phil.

Beyond that, though, is the fact that Phil is a kind wise man with a generous manly personality, and I admire and love his gentle way with me. He's a good man.

The third reason Phil is important to me is that Phil loves me and to be loved is a special thing that I yearn for even now.

2007

"You're a treasure, Debbie," Phil said as I got out the Christmas stuff to play with. He meant that I always have projects and plans and the joy to do them.

2008

I miss Phil. We are such constant friends that it's very quiet and lonely in my heart right now, as I fear he'll be going away forever.

He has beaten certain death at least three times now, with the empyema and then double pneumonia, and then the abdomen operation, so it is easy to let myself be hopeful that once again he'll be back with me. And there are hopeful signs he's getting stronger each day.

My Phil. Our love for each other has been a true and wonderful thing.

***

Yesterday I visited Phil. The doctor told us he can't be operated on for three months due to the heart attack he had last time. So he is going to live in the nursing home unit at the VA hospital for three months.

Now's when I get lonely and empty, as the day ends. No

Phil sitting nearby to talk to, to tease, to nag, to hug, to just be with. And it feels like no one else will do. He shouldn't be my everything, but he is a good part of my everything.

Something pulling at my heart. Sadness.

***

I just now cried awhile on the sofa, felt so lonely and sad. I told myself to put the feeling into words, and the words that came to me were, "I want Phil." Like a child crying for Mama or Daddy. Every time I said I want Phil to myself, I cried again and again. Feel sad even now with tears. Why do I have to go along without my Phil? I wish he wasn't so sick. Somehow I wish death didn't exist. But I don't get my wishes. It feels like I never do get a wish, even a reasonable one.

That's not true. I have love. I was given someone to love and I was given someone who loves me just as much.

***

(After Phil's death) I want my Phil back again. Yesterday as I waited in the store for Mama's medicines, I thought of how when Phil and I were in the store, and we'd go off on our own, and then to see him walking down the aisle toward me, my heart would lift. We were almost always in love, the "in love" sort of love, not just the old comfy sort of love.

***

I thought about Phil as usual last night, how we'd go to bed side by side and he'd put his arm around me and pull me tight to his body. I miss that every time I lie down. Oh, my man.

"Oh, My Redwood Heart!"

***

I'm tired, tired. I want Phil. I want Phil. Oh, how I want Phil. His love. His company. His gentleness. His smile. His contentment. His hands. His smell. His naked body. His soft curls. His hug so close. His soft kiss. His hard kiss. His voice in my ears. I want his all, his everything.

***

On my way into town I listened to music on the radio. I thought about the songs Phil and I had liked, the old one from *South Pacific*, "Some Enchanted Evening;" the song from the *Phantom of the Opera*; and the western sounding song "Stuck on You," with the words, "Mighty glad you stayed." Each song brought its memories to me, how in the early part of our marriage we'd sing "..if you have found her, never let her go…(or him)" and later when Phil came back from his year in the Iowa Domiciliary, at the busy airport our eyes "met across a crowded room." How in 1988-89 we lived in Gridley and had the furniture store and a neat little house, the president's celebration was on TV and when Michael Crawford sang "Music of the Night," Phil and I both stopped and stayed still to listen, how the next day we went shopping for the record. And then how whenever Phil stayed home instead of going on a trip, or whenever Phil realized I'd stayed with him through a lot of hard times one or the other of us would sing, "Mighty glad you stayed," from "Stuck on You." Tears flowed as all these memories went through my mind.

***

I've been thinking of Phil a lot today. My heart is sore. Why can't I have my Phil back? Death is mean.
My man. My dear. My best one. To think of your face.

213

To think of touching you, stroking your hair, rubbing your shoulders, lying in your arms. If only you were here to hold me while I cry.

Dearest Phil of my heart.

***

This afternoon I decided to test the CD player in my new car, so I took "Dances with Wolves" out. The tone of the speakers was so much richer than my stereo in the house that the music sounded beautiful. When I tuned the CD to "The John Dunbar theme" I was overcome with emotions about Phil. I cried hard. I put the song on again and gave into my sobbing. The music went far into me, expanding into all that was Phil to me. That particular song is western, big sky, encompassing nature and adventure, and suffering, too. Sadness missing my Phil. I also played the song of Two Socks the wolf, which was lighter, more playful, and I made that song me and the first song Phil, and thought how we fit together like the music.

I know I'm remembering mostly the good and loving and wise of Phil, not the troubled or irritating of Phil, but truly I loved him and loved being with him, my best friend, my man. Oh how can I live without his arms holding me? I can just feel them going around me. Strong warm with Phil's manly smell around me, around me. My dearest man of mine... there's a sad little bird inside me.

But, the little bird knows Phil is gone, buried in the casket under the earth out on the Nevada desert where the rabbits race and the coyotes yip.

2009

I miss joy. The joy of having someone to tease and laugh and play with. I'm not brave enough to be free enough to be my joyful self with anyone. Only Phil saw the happiest of me. I wish I could be free and fun with others.

I want more than I can have. I must try to accept the faultiness of life. I'm shy. Most likely I'll always be shy. I had love. I may never have love again. But I had it once.

***

Driving my way home in the blowing snow, I began to miss Phil and cried about him. Tears ran down my cheeks. I had a new vision of Phil, thinking of him as a young man, a man, an individual being, a human. I thought of him more as he was without me included -- a separate man with a brain full of his own being. That thought made me sob -- oh, how can a person so complete, so real, so valuable, so individual, be gone, gone forever. I felt I could understand the need to believe in an afterlife. I wished I could at that moment. It would be a comfort.

***

Thinking of the first time and the last time Phil and I made love - makes me smile, how the first time Phil had to instruct me, which was funny, and the last time when Phil didn't stay long enough, and we finished with touchy hands, which was just as good for me, anyway.

I like to think of the other loving times, too, when we were both satisfied. I loved Phil's warm manliness. I loved how we loved. How we laughed at our foibles sometimes. I wish I could have Phil back somehow, as well and strong as he was at his best.

2010

A memory came to me when I saw a neighbor outside opening his car trunk. I just remembered how I'd see Phil from a distance, me in the house and he at the car, how I'd love seeing him without him knowing I was watching. Because then it felt like I could see him as a whole separate person, with a big big life inside him, so beautiful and poignant, too, knowing all his dreams and troubles.

***

After a nap today, I looked in the Memory book in the shelf of my nightstand. I haven't read all the things about Phil I gathered for people at the funeral to look at and sign for a long time. Tears began to flow. I'm filled with the realization of the richness of my life, how much I've experienced, how gifts of love have been given to me.

***

Saw on TV an actor hugging the actress who played his fiancé. His hug enveloped her like Phil's hug enveloped me. Phil's hug wasn't just a hug, it was warm and complete, full of love and protection. Then I put my head up and cried, howled like a lonely wolf (softly). Out in the night alone alone, whimpering -- Oooooo. My heart suffers.

***

Looking at the silver chain that hangs from my lamp switch - it was Phil's necklace on which he kept his locker key at the VA nursing unit those last days of his life. It has charms, a silver heart, a silver padlock and key, and a peace symbol dangling from it, and now also holds my gold wedding ring. But my memory shows me the necklace swinging on Phil's neck, across the hairs of his chest. All the intense love and care, pity and yearning I had for him in that last year of his life, into the last week and days, his last words to me, "You know I love you," after I'd kissed him gently on the forehead - that's what my memory shows me, as I feel on my palm the silver pieces slipping with the gold.

❧Goodbye, Phil ❧
Epilogue, 2016

Sometimes I miss the softly feathered pigeon friends we used to keep in the backyard. RolyPoly, so handsome in red and white, I wonder how his life continued after I gave him to another pigeon fancier in the area. With RolyPoly went his shy wife UpsyDaisy, and to other Birmingham Roller fans went SkyRoller, TopsyTurvy, my favorite feisty hen, RoundAbout, and all the others. Perhaps there are generations of the P & D Coop rollers still rolling and swooping in the skies of Reno.

Almost eight years it has been. Each anniversary of Phil's death I've gone to town, to the 7/11 above where the Wagon Wheel Motel property used to be. I pass the straight and dark forest-green redwoods that line the parking lot pavement where once stood our family compound, and I pull up to the store that Phil went to daily for his treats when we used to live and love in our drafty Hill House in the 90s. There I buy a package of mini powdered doughnuts and a bottle of chocolate milk, just what I used to like when Phil and I went to the Park back then. And I drive to San Rafael Park, across the highway, and settle in our regular place overlooking the Arboretum. How these trees have grown, too, the English Oaks that were planted as children along the rise of a grassy hill by the entrance; now they are young adults in tree life, and in August they are shady green and spotted sunlight.

"Oh, My Redwood Heart!"

All this I see for my eyes, and for my ears I put on the car CD player - *John Dunbar's theme* from *Dances with Wolves*, which is a sound portrait of Phil to me. Some years I've cried, and some I've smiled and remembered. One year I sang my own song to the music, about living, seeing beauty, about realizing the great expanse of space there is to fill in the openings of the mind. Histories of love, of thoughts and inventions, lives of others, from those you meet once to those you love forever, and one whole life of your own, all this and more fit into the universe of the brain. And my song was also about how preciously fragile the brain's universe and the human's life can be, nature-made from the beginning and subject to infinitesimal pluses and minuses of health and chance. So many elements go into the making of a life that it hurts to know. And it hurts to know the end brings death, always. But death takes care of itself, and it is wonderful to let it go, to be free and to live my one life as a rare, a singular! treasure. Be good, be kind, love, and be loved, that's what I sang to myself.

These few years I've lived as a widow in my Aldebaran House, wishing some new gentleman would fall into my life, but going on as usual anyway. Old Jenny, who still likes to lie on the spot where once she felt safe under Phil's legs as he sat on the couch - she still shakes up the household and claims top dog status. William the conquering cat died, but I adopted an orphan kitten, smoky black Finnigan. Chamois, the little Himalayan cat, named by Phil, she's still here, too, drifting like a tiny white cloud around the house. My mom, now 92, has a little dog we call Sunshine. Then soon after Phil's death, I came across an online request for someone to adopt a golden doodle dog that wasn't given enough attention. I call him PJ, short for Phil's Jasper, Jasper because that was the name Phil thought of for a pet in his last days. My PJ - this curly-red-haired dog with the warm brown eyes has helped me by being as sweet as Phil and not letting me get too sad. He's good for hugging, too.

The last time I sobbed really hard about Phil was a couple of years ago, when I rented a Peter O'Toole movie called *Venus*. O'Toole plays an old man who falls in love with a young woman who comes to stay with him, and then she loves him, and eventually takes care of him in his last illness. Phil even looked like Peter O'Toole did in that movie, with the rectangular bony face, the stretched smile, the tall thinness caught in a wheelchair. Meanwhile the young woman, though much wilder and younger than I, reminded me of my pure love and the cheeriness, or playfulness, I felt around my man. I know I'm getting too mushy, but this is the end of my tale.

Goodbye, my Phil, I'm singing. Goodbye, my redwood-hearted man. Goodbye, my Phil, goodbye, goodbye.

"Oh, My Redwood Heart!"